James,
Good Luck

GARDEN PROJECTS FOR RUFFIANS

A ROUGH & READY GUIDE TO GARDEN MAKEOVERS

By Phil Thane

The Good Life Press LTD

GARDEN PROJECTS FOR RUFFIANS

Published by The Good Life Press Ltd. 2011

ISBN 978 1 90487 1941

A catalogue record for this book is available from
the British Library.

Published by
The Good Life Press Ltd.
The Old Pigsties
Clifton Fields
Lytham Road
Preston
PR4 0XG

www.goodlifepress.co.uk
www.homefarmer.co.uk

Cover design by Fat Giraffe Graphics
www.fatgiraphics.com

CONTENTS

FOREWORD

Not a Show Garden, not a TV Show. This is real.

Show gardens are not real. They are faked at huge expense using imported soil, elaborate features and the best plants a team of dedicated professionals can produce, given a year to prepare and greenhouses measured in hectares.

Reality TV is anything but real. Houses and gardens featured in makeover shows are selected to make good TV. The gardens are mostly flat, have easy access for hordes of builders and gardeners with a truck-load of power tools, and a very big budget.

Gardening books are full of photos of gardens that bear no relation at all to the patch we own, and take it for granted that we have very deep pockets. This book is for those whose garden is an impenetrable mix of rock and weeds and whose financial priorities don't include spending several grand on a water feature. It's about making the best of what you've got, throwing away nothing and spending very little.

MEASUREMENTS

The metric system is used worldwide by all engineering, building and manufacturing industries, and by almost everyone for everyday measurements too. One notable exception is the UK where 40 years ago the government botched it. Subsequent governments, scared of the conflation of metrication and Euroscepticism in the mass media, have ducked the issue ever since.

Metrication causes particular problems for writers. Since metric usage is grudging at best, metric terms haven't entered the general vocabulary and phrases like 'an inch or two', or 'a couple of feet' are still widely used, whereas saying 'fifty mil' (or writing 50mm) raises eyebrows.

I normally use metric and have done since I took A' level engineering in metric in 1970 (I did O' levels two years earlier using imperial). Most measurements in this book are approximate; that's why it's a 'rough & ready guide' so slavish conversions to the nearest thousandth of an inch or milligram would be ridiculous. I give measurements in metric with rough equivalents for those who haven't been paying attention for 40 years, but slip in the odd vernacular reference to 'three by two' timbers.

CHAPTER 1

SOIL (OR LACK OF IT)

Soil is the basis for most gardens; unless you have a yen for Japanese gravel or crave a concrete car park you need soil to grow things. Given how essential it is, it does seem to be strangely absent from many gardens. Our first house was a two-up, two down that had been modernised and extended. The modernisation involved knocking through downstairs and the extension involved opening up holes in the back wall. So there was a lot of rubble which the previous owner had dumped in the back garden and left until the weeds hid it from view.

Then we had a house in Lancashire with a back garden based on a century's worth of cinders from the fire, followed by a newer house in Cambridgeshire where the builders had removed the topsoil and laid turf like cheap carpet to hide the subsoil.

Builders don't like topsoil as it turns to mud when it rains and sticks to their machines and their boots and if it gets really wet it slides around and they lose track of where ground level is supposed to be. So the first stage of most building projects is to scrape it all off. There was a time when they heaped it up at the side of the site, then put it back when they'd finished but these days land is so expensive they have to squeeze another house onto the site rather than waste space storing soil. The soil is taken away, sieved, sterilised, bagged and sold in DIY stores to people that have just bought a house with no soil in the garden!

And then we moved to North Wales. People that have lived round here a long time say our garden used to be beautiful, but as so often happens the owners got old and couldn't maintain it, then they died and there was an unseemly squabble over inheritance and the place became derelict. Eventually a young guy bought it to restore and sell on.

The restoration work on the house was pretty average but the real tragedy was the garden. He hired a digger and carved up what had been a steep slope divided by ancient walls into three levels. The proper way to do this is to remove the topsoil, landscape the subsoil, build retaining walls and then put the topsoil back.

BEFORE

AFTER

Gardening doesn't come rougher than this.

But he only had the digger for a day. He dug into the hillside and shovelled the subsoil and rock on top of the topsoil. The result was unstable; the old walls couldn't take the extra weight and started to lean and the rocky subsoil started to slide off the old topsoil level in a slow motion landslip. It was so unstable that no-one could get a mortgage on the property until a very ugly concrete wall was built behind the house. Not just any old wall either: it had to be designed by a civil engineer, built by specialists and given a 25 year guarantee. This engineering saved the house, but when we moved in it was only the weeds, by then taller than me, which were holding the rest of the garden in place.

You can become obsessed by soil. Let's start with a few quick tips for gardening with very little of the stuff.

GRASS

Grass will grow on almost anything, which is how builders get away with 'carpeting' round new builds with turf. If you hanker after a bowling green or a tennis lawn you will need perfect soil but if you just want a green space for a sunlounger and a barbie, an inch or two of poor soil with most of the rocks removed will do.

The lawn on the left was actually hacked from bedrock with a pickaxe. Fortunately the rock is a sort of dirty mudstone that crumbles very easily, so we were able to remove all the pieces big enough to pick up and blended the smaller stuff with soil from elsewhere in the garden and finally seeded it. It's by no means a great lawn.

It has moss in the winter, primroses in the spring and dandelions in the summer. From time to time another stone still comes to the surface and knocks the edge off the lawnmower blade, but the fact it's there at all is satisfaction enough.

PLANTING POCKETS

Wisteria doing well in Cambridge clay.

Cambridgeshire is in an area renowned for its sand, gravel and clay pits. True to form the builders of this new estate removed all the topsoil, so what remains is a sticky mix of sand, gravel and clay. Replacing all the topsoil would be way too expensive, but it's amazing how well many plants will do planted in 'pockets'.

The basic idea is to dig a hole about as big as you expect the fully grown plant to be, fill it with decent soil and plant into that. In this case the subsoil is a pretty good mix of aggregates, but is totally lacking in any organic matter, so we just removed all the larger stones, mixed a lot of compost into the soil from the hole and replaced it.

The result a couple of years later is that most of the plants are doing really well. The shrubs in particular have powerful roots and once established they can break out of the pocket and into the subsoil. Softer plants may not manage this but providing the pocket is big enough they don't really seem to mind.

We use pockets in Llan too. Here we had to use a pick to dig a hole in the lawn for a honeysuckle. The turf went in the bottom of the hole, followed by some decent soil

Rocks removed, homemade compost going in.

from the compost heap and the honeysuckle is doing well. Hopefully it will hide the gabion in a few years.

Pockets don't even have to be in the ground. This bit of wall is all that remains of an old cottage, retained as a buttress to our neighbour's house. The owner has strengthened it a little by cementing some of the stones back in place, but left pockets and filled them with compost for creeping plants to get a hold. They only went in a few weeks before the photo but they should look great in a year or two.

Plants soften a rough wall.

CONTAINERS

Unless you have a very formal classical garden with perfectly judged specimens, one or two plants in pots can look a bit sad. A massed rank of different containers looks a lot better, and you can move them around and hide the ones that are finished, or never really got started. Posh pots from garden centres are expensive but a mix'n'match selection of terracotta pots, buckets, chimney pots and plastic containers looks informal and fun. In trendy parts of London it's smart (they tell me) to use catering size virgin olive oil cans. They don't seem to exist outside the M25, though.

A mix'n'match collection of containers make the most of a narrow bed.

Unless you are growing bog plants your containers will need a hole or two to prevent them becoming waterlogged. A hot piece of steel such as a fire poker will go through plastic nicely, but do it outside as the fumes are not nice. A sharp spike, chisel or screwdriver will go through most tin can bases with a bit of a tap from a hammer. Watch the edges though as they'll be sharp. Galvanised steel buckets look good, but you'll need a power drill to make holes in them.

Tumbler toms growing well in containers.

Put a few bits of brick, stone, slate or broken flowerpot over the holes and fill the containers up with soil or compost. The tumbler tomatoes are doing well in chimney pots full of compost, outdoors. in North Wales.

BAGS OF THE STUFF

If you've been building for a while you'll soon have a collection of 'tonne bags' (sometimes called 'dumpy bags') that builders' merchants use to deliver aggregates. If you've been gardening for a while or even just hacking down weeds, you'll have a heap of compost. Maybe not great compost but shovel it into a bag and you'll have an instant 'raised bed'. This one is on a rocky slope that normally grows only grass and dandelions, but it produced a fine crop of spuds.

Potatoes like a lot of nutrients so kitchen waste compost added to the mix is useful and normal garden compost, leaf mould and even a bit of soil if you can spare it can all go in the bag. Poke a few holes in the bag with a garden fork to stop it getting waterlogged. Put about a foot (30cm) of soil/compost in and plant five or six spuds about 15cm deep. It's easier if you fold down the top of the bag as per the photo.

Old spuds starting to sprout.

You can buy seed potatoes, and should if you're serious about growing potatoes, but these are just old spuds that had been left in the kitchen too long and started to

Earth up the spuds regularly.

Spuds nearly ready to harvest.

sprout. Plant them in early April and a month later they'll be out of the soil and growing strongly. Bags like this warm up quicker than the earth and that encourages things to grow. Make sure the soil keeps moist as once the plants are fully grown their leaves tend to form an effective umbrella that diverts most of the rainfall out of the bag.

Once the plants are about 20cm high, shovel some more soil/compost in until only about 5-10cm of the stalks and leaves are visible.

Repeat this whenever the plants get about 15cm high, probably 3-4 times during the summer, unfolding the sides of the bag as you go. 'Earthing up' like this stops the sunlight getting to the tubers and making them go green. It also encourages the plants to make more tubers so by the autumn you should have a bag full of spuds.

You've also got a bag full of soil you can use elsewhere – but don't use it for potatoes again as it can harbour disease that might attack next year's crop.

These bags have been folded over to make shallower beds ready for strawberry runners. They are on the rocky slope where the potatoes were, but notice the rudimentary platform on the left to keep them level. It's just pallet boards driven in to the ground, nailed together and backfilled with rock.

More on uses for 'tonne' bags, and compost making later...

Next year's strawberry crop.

STONES (AND BRICKS) ARE NOT RUBBISH

Gardening on a hillside is mostly about moving stones around. Stone is heavy so the trick is not to move it far. Initially this will probably mean heaps of the things all over the place, until you work out what to do with them. Big stones obviously go into walls and flat stones make paths, steps or caps on top of those walls. Even the small stuff can be used. If you are building 'rubble' walls you will need rubble to fill them and stuff too small for even that can go into concrete, foundations for sheds and so on. The strawberry beds above are resting on stones removed when we built a path.

Bricks are not necessarily rubbish either. You can use them for walls, possibly for paving, or just as hardcore beneath sheds or concrete. Old bricks nicely cleaned up go for 50p each on Ebay! The brick wall on page 30 was built entirely from recycled bricks.

MAKING YOUR OWN SOIL

Compost heaps, both old and new.

Composting

Despite what you might think it isn't magic. If you pile up any kind of 'biomass' it will eventually rot. Composting is just organising the process so you get a useful soil improver in a reasonable period of time. There aren't any definitive rules but a few tips might help:

- *Mix the stuff you put in. Grass clippings will make a slimy layer if a lot are piled in together, but mixed with leafier stuff and kitchen waste they rot fine.*
- *Don't try to compost prunings from shrubs/trees unless you have a shredder to chew them up first. Even small twigs take years to rot. If you don't have a shredder, burn them and sprinkle the ashes on the heap instead.*
- *Even sturdy flower stems need chopping. Put them on the ground and chop them with a sharp spade.*
- *Turning the compost every few weeks will help it rot evenly.*
- *If turning isn't practical have two heaps. Make one and leave it a year. Take the top off and use it to start the next heap. The stuff underneath will probably be usable.*
- *Keep the heap moist and if it's sited under trees it will need watering occasionally. Even an exposed heap can dry out if there is no rain for a couple of weeks. Older gardeners have been known to pee on their compost. I couldn't possibly comment.*
- *Don't be tempted to add pet poo as it will stink. Bedding straw from small pet cages seems OK though.*
- *If you have a very active, hot compost heap it will destroy seeds and even perennial roots, however ruffian compost heaps don't, so it's a good idea not to compost things like dandelion roots.*
- *Problem weeds will die if you leave them out on a paved area with no soil and no water, but dehydrating dandelions on your patio is not a good look. My alternative is to stuff them in an old sand or cement bag with a handful of lime and leave them until they look very, very dead. Then compost them.*

Kitchen waste is great in a compost heap, but don't put meat in as it will smell terrible. Veg and fruit peelings, stalks, outer leaves and even teabags are OK. Crushed egg shells add grit, which is fine. Some gardeners advise you to avoid citrus fruit peel due its acidity, but unless you make your own orange juice in vast quantities it's not a problem. Chop up the peel and sling it in.[1] Rhubarb leaves are OK too. The poisonous oxalic acid in them is destroyed as they decompose.

[1] *If your main compost heap is far from the kitchen a closed composter is useful near the house. A 'green bin' in the kitchen to collect stuff is useful, and surprisingly un-smelly.*

It's easier to turn compost if you build your heap on a smooth flat base. At Kew they have a huge concrete yard with compost heaps the size of a house that they turn with a JCB, but it's not essential - you can build a heap on the ground.

Left to its own devices a heap will spread. It will always work better if it's constrained in a bin of some sort. Left uncovered compost will start to grow its own cover as perennial weed roots and opportunistic seeds start to sprout. There is also a danger that the heap will get too wet or too dry depending on the weather. You'll get more compost, and quicker if you have some sort of cover. An old carpet or yet another tonne bag will do, but a proper hinged lid is better. See chapter 8 for how to build compost bins.

Rough compost made like this is OK for raised beds or for just improving the soil, but if you want to use it for potting or growing seeds it will need sieving. See pages 72-73 for a homemade soil sieve.

Leaf Mould

Mouldering leaves.

You can add small quantities of autumn leaves to a compost heap but if you have a lot of trees there is a better way. Leaf mould is the stuff that makes up most of the soil in woodland and if you make your own it's ideal for mulching around woodland plants. There are very few nutrients in leaf mould, but it does improve soil structure and improves water retention in sandy soils.

- Rake up the leaves and pile them into a bin bag, or if you have enough, a 'tonne bag'.
- Poke a few holes in the bag so it doesn't become totally waterlogged.
- Make sure the leaves are damp, water if necessary then tie up the bag and leave it for a year.

Bark/woodchip

If you saw up your own firewood you will soon be ankle deep in sawdust and bark. You can add some to a compost heap, especially if you have a kitchen

Mulched with a mix of rotted sawdust and bark.

waste composter that is very wet. If you have too much for that, collect it in plastic bags and leave it to get wet, then fold the tops over and stack them out of the way for a year or two. Composted bark makes a good mulch round fruit bushes. Composted sawdust isn't so pretty, but the bushes don't seem to mind. A mix of leaves, bark and sawdust works well too.

LANDSCAPING AND PLANNING

In general I disapprove of 'landscaping'. Artificial hills and valleys look artificial unless you are working on several hectares of parkland. If you already have a hill some sympathetic terracing does make it easier to work, just don't make the mistake our predecessor made and bury your topsoil!

I'm not keen on too much planning either. Obviously you need an idea of what you are aiming for but gardens are four dimensional; to plan one in detail you would need sophisticated 3D modelling and a means of showing how the plants will change over time.

Make a start by assessing what you have, and what's worth keeping. It makes sense to work on the area nearest the house first as it's the part you and your visitors will see most and it's good to have somewhere tidy to sprawl out when you're worn out. If your plot is overgrown you are going to need big compost heaps to take all of the weeds you're going to dig up, so finding somewhere to put them is a very good first step. Out of sight if possible, but reasonably accessible.

Even badly neglected gardens often retain some interesting features, and plants can survive years of neglect. You might decide you can restore and tidy without starting anew. If that's out of the question it might be worth clearing a small area to use as a 'holding bed' for any plants you find that you want to keep. Ideally have it in the area you plan to do last so you don't have to move things around too often.

Annual plants will often self-seed if neglected and pop up in the most unlikely places. If you do find something interesting wait until the seed pods develop and harvest the seed. Keep it in paper envelopes so you can reseed the plot once you've cleared and tidied it. Real gardeners label their seed envelopes in Latin but Anglo-Saxon descriptions will do to remind you what's what.

Some terraces are narrow and high.

TERRACES can be narrow, each only a few centimetres higher than its neighbour or wider and higher. Narrow terraces will need a lot more walls building, but each wall can be simpler since it supports less. Wide terraces need a lot of digging, and require big strong walls to support them, but if you live on a mountainside it's the only way to make room for a shed, a garage, an office or a lawn. See chapter 3 for building new garden walls.

In this case it's decking or nothing.

DECKING got a bad name in the 1990s when it was used to cover vast areas of suburban garden, but it does have a sensible purpose when your land is so steep your sun lounger thinks it's a toboggan.

Plants will grow in steeply sloping ground, but gardeners tend to fall over. When the shrubbery overleaf was being planted we built temporary paths by banging old roof timbers into the ground and laying floorboards against them. By the time the wood had rotted the shrubs were established and the soil much more secure.

If you do have steeply sloping ground, build lots of steps. It's infuriating to be at the right end of the plot but on the wrong level with the only way up or down involving a long walk to the other end. If the plot has only a modest slope then build ramps, they're much better for wheelbarrows. If you are starting new terraces on a steep slope consider making each one slope a little and link them to create a zig-zag route for wheelbarrows, and add short cut steps for gardeners in a hurry.

You need steps, and temporary paths while planting.

CHAPTER 2

DODGY WALLS

Old walls have a unique charm; the unevenness, the cracked mortar and the lichen and moss which mature over many years. And shortly after that they start to fall down. If you want to keep an old wall, and it's much cheaper than pulling it down and starting again, then you need to maintain it.

SURVEY

You don't need qualifications to survey your own garden walls, a spirit level, a pair of eyes and a bit of common sense will do. Here's a checklist:

1. Is it standing upright? Not always easy to tell with random stone walls. Place a board against it to average out the minor lumps and bumps and use a spirit level on the board. If it's leaning it's going to be very difficult to correct so unless there are planning/conservation issues it probably needs replacing.
2. Is it cracked? Cracks in individual bricks or stones or short sections of mortar line are insignificant. Long cracks running down a wall suggest the foundations are inadequate, and once again you might have to rebuild it. Horizontal cracks can occur in retaining walls that are not up to the job and are starting to move.
3. Is anything growing out of it? Climbing plants rooted in the earth below a wall are rarely a problem, hanging plants growing in the ground behind a retaining wall and dangling over it are pretty harmless too, the danger comes from things like shrubs and trees that take root in cracks and steadily demolish the wall as they grow.
4. Does it need repointing? Rough rule of thumb; it does if lumps of mortar are falling out, or if the average depth of the mortar line is greater than the width. Pointing is mind-numbing and slow, but it's not particularly difficult and makes the wall look better and last a lot longer.
5. Does it have a secure 'cap'? The top of a wall is vulnerable to water, frost and plant growth. Capping takes many forms: stone, concrete/ reconstituted stone, terracotta or even mortar. What ever it is it needs to be sound.

DEAL WITH IT

If your wall fails points 1 or 2 you're probably going to be rebuilding at least part of it, so see Chapter 3 - New Walls.

If you have anything actually growing in the wall (point 3 above) get it out immediately and point the hole up to stop anything else getting in there (below). If it's growing in the top get it out and fix the capping (even further below).

POINTING

When bricklayers and masons build walls they smooth the mortar line with the tip of their trowel as they go. Gradually the mortar breaks down under the assault of wind and rain and the surface retreats. This erosion of the mortar line creates nooks and crannies for water to seep in, for dirt to lodge and seeds to take root and hastens the general decay of the wall. It needs doing before things get worse.

Preparation

There's no point slapping new mortar on loose, crumbly stuff as it will just fall out after a year or two. You need to rake out the loose stuff at least as deep as the mortar line is wide. Even where the mortar is good you need to get back that far to ensure a good key. An old screwdriver or chisel will usually do the job, unless you have fine mortar lines on a brick wall made from 'facing' or engineering bricks. These are harder, shiny and slightly larger than common bricks and the mortar lines are thinner. They aren't common in gardens but you do see them around early 20th century houses. If it really needs doing an angle grinder is the easiest way, but noisy and dusty. Don't forget the safety gear too!

Dig out the old mortar as deep as the joins are wide – which can be a long way!

Don't prepare a huge area. Pointing is slow and boring and you'll probably get rained off or find something more interesting to do before you've replaced it all. Hack out a square metre or so and point it immediately. Hopefully it will look better and encourage you to do a bit more.

Brush out the joints to remove any dust and fragments then spray with water before you apply any new mortar. If the wall is bone dry it will suck the water out of the mortar before it has a chance to react with the cement. The water also creates a thin layer of extra-sloppy mortar next to the brick/stone which makes sure you get a good bond. Don't overdo it though or the whole lot gets sloppy and falls out!

Making mortar with lime putty and sharp sand.

Mortars

Mortar is made from aggregate mixed with either cement or lime, sometimes both. Cement is cheaper and is used more sparingly so is well suited to ruffian work. Lime is 'greener' in that it takes less energy to make it, and lime mortar is softer.

Soft mortar might not seem like a good idea, but it can be in some situations. Walls move a little as the temperature changes and a softer mortar accommodates this. If you build with cement you should leave an expansion gap every few metres. If you are building with soft old common bricks and a hard cement mortar, the bricks may well crack when the wall moves.

Repointing an old wall built with lime mortar using cement mortar is common, but not usually very successful. The old mortar will 'give' a little and the cement won't and after a few hot summers and cold winters the cement falls out.

Lime mortar looks more appropriate if you are restoring an old wall or building a new one adjacent to an old one. In conservation areas it is usually compulsory, and the conservation officer will probably even dictate the colour of sand you use and the precise mix. But ruffians don't live in conservation areas, do they? For detailed mixes see the table on page 108.

Whatever mix you are using, make up a small amount, especially if you are doing brickwork with narrow mortar lines. Make too much and it will 'go off' before you've used it. If you are using lime mortar on a rubble stone wall it's a different matter, though as you'll need a lot and it stays usable longer, providing you keep it damp.

Tools

For brickwork you need a small pointing trowel to apply the mortar and something flat to hold a dollop of it close to the wall (and to catch bits that fall out too!). A plasterer's 'float' is OK if you are fiddling around with small quantities on a brick wall but a 'hawk' is better if you need more. You can make a hawk from a piece of plywood about a foot square nailed to a piece of rounded wood

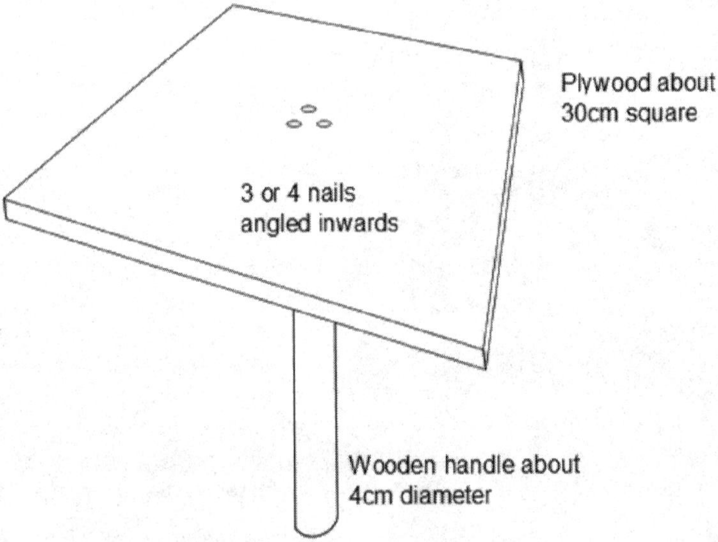

Wider mortar lines in stone work can be tackled with a bricklaying trowel, but I confess that for years I've used an old curved garden trowel when pointing (and building) rubble walls. It scoops up mortar easily and the back of it gives a slightly concave finish to the pointing.

Cement and lime are bad for the skin and at the very least your hands will feel rough for days afterwards if you don't wear gloves. Heavy duty gardening gloves are ideal for most building work. When repairing rubble stone walls I use PVC-dipped cotton gloves, the sort you might keep for unblocking drains, and apply the mortar by taking a handful and slapping it or throwing it into the holes!

Application

On brick walls take a small amount of mortar on the edge of a trowel and press it in. Repeat the process and every few rows stop and smooth what you've done.

If you are using a conventional diamond trowel, hold it with the handle lower than the joint and use a long side to smooth the mortar, leaving the surface sloping back slightly. Do the vertical lines first, then the horizontal ones from the top down. This should result in each mortar line ending slightly 'proud' of the one beneath to throw off water. If you do it the other way up you create pockets to catch water. It makes more sense once you've tried it.

A ruffian alternative is 'round' pointing finished off with a special steel tool, a piece of 15mm copper pipe or even a stick.

On rough stone walls the process is correspondingly rougher. Whatever tool you use the object is to get the mortar deep into the joint. Trowel the surface roughly smooth and leave it until the mortar is firm but not solid, then brush it gently with a hand brush to smooth the surface, leaving it slightly concave between the stones.

If you have posh regular stones, treat them like bricks and remember that cement stains many types of brick and stone, so try to keep the mortar off the surface as much as possible.

Slap the mortar well in and smooth it later.

CAPPING

The point of capping a wall is to keep water out, but we've got so accustomed to seeing capped walls they look unfinished without. Except round here funnily enough, where it's quite common to finish rubble stone walls by just cementing some flattish stones on top.

No capping, just flattish stones and plenty of cement.

Common bricks are porous and if they absorb water then freeze, the surface is blown off by the expanding ice. Brick walls are often capped with stone slabs, concrete or 'reconstituted stone' slabs or better quality waterproof bricks. Whatever you use the gaps should be as small as possible and well pointed to keep the water out.

Stone walls often have stone slab capping too, but the artificial stone that works OK on brick walls looks particularly horrid up against the real thing. Where larger pieces of random stone occur you often see walls capped alternately with large and small pieces, or pieces of similar size. Arrange one flat, the next upright and so on. Either way you get a castellated appearance.

A common dodge to extend the life of old dry stone walls is to slap on a cap of rough lime mortar. It binds the top layer together and keeps the rain out. A slightly more modern variation is to use concrete, either a dryish mix applied freehand or by rigging up some simple shuttering and pouring a slab on top of the wall.

CHAPTER 3

NEW WALLS

MATERIALS

Building materials are expensive and rarely appear on Freecycle. The cheapest are grey concrete blocks which look pretty terrible unless you render and paint them, so wherever possible the ruffian gardener recycles whatever he/she can find.

Old walls built with lime mortar fall down quite readily and the mortar cleans off the bricks or stones without too much trouble, so keep an eye out for local demolition work. Big developers are unlikely to help as 'Elf 'n' Safety' won't let you on the site and they will have policies on recycling, the safe removal of materials and heaven knows what else. A small builder might be more helpful, but friends pulling down old extensions, chimney stacks and outbuildings are a better bet. Best of all are materials you've already got from your own projects.

Bricks

UK bricks used to be made on a 9" module, the idea being that one brick plus one mortar line was 9" long, two bricks sideways with two mortar lines, or three bricks on edge with three mortar lines was also 9". Common bricks were smaller and uneven and a wider mortar line was used to accommodate them.

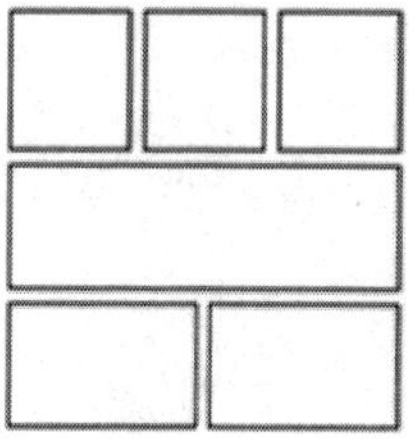

Three bricks on edge or two bricks sideways equals one brick width (with mortar lines)

Engineering bricks and facing bricks were larger and more regular and used less mortar, but because they used the same module you could use engineering bricks for the foundations, commons for the bulk of the wall and facing bricks for the corners and capping and everything would still fit. Then we went metric. UK Metric bricks are made on a 225mm module, which is a bit less than 9" though you can mix and match them by using a bit of extra mortar.

Facing bricks usually have indentations on each face (called frogs) so that you get a good joint even with very thin mortar lines. Some bricks have frogs only on one side, in which case the rule is 'down with frogs'.

If you are using recycled bricks, try to collect them all first and group them according to type. Count what you've got and figure out a design to make good use of them. For small walls you'll know almost exactly what you'll need and for larger projects work on about 60 per square metre for a single skin wall.

The biggest problem with old bricks is cleaning off the old mortar. Lime mortar isn't too difficult and can usually be knocked off with the edge of a trowel, especially if the bricks have been left out in the rain for a while. Bricks from newer properties built with cement are very difficult. If they are really special and worth the effort you're going to need a cold chisel, a hammer and a lot of time.

Bricks come in a wide range of colours. Until quite recently people just made bricks from local clay and all the buildings around looked the same. Then cities got too big for that and bricks were brought in from all around and the colours varied. Then the 'designers' got involved and now every new development in the land uses a range of remarkably similar colours.

If you reuse old bricks from your neighbourhood they will look OK in an old garden. If you have a more modern house and garden you should probably try to find bricks to match, or at least not clash too horribly.

Concrete Bricks (Building)

Concrete bricks are an alternative to clay bricks. They are strong, cheap and can look stylish in modern buildings, but most are rendered and/or painted. Their use in bricking up the windows in derelict houses has done nothing for their image.

Concrete Bricks (Paviors)

Ordinary common bricks are not water resistant. If you use them for paving or capping walls the surface will absorb water. During the winter that water will freeze and as ice is about 10% bigger than the water it's made from, the surface will be blown off. In Victorian times paving made from engineering bricks, usually blue or chunky tiles made from the same blue clay, was quite common but the bricks and tiles are fiercely expensive now. 'Paviors' made from concrete are a cheaper alternative: the trouble is, they look it.

Frost damage to brick paving.

Stone

Until railways were built in the nineteenth century, stone was always local. Apart from the occasional royal or aristo who could afford to pay huge amounts to ship and cart more fashionable rocks to build his latest palace, everyone made the best of what was available. In many places that's some form of 'mudstone', halfway between limestone and shale. It breaks into unpredictable size pieces with very few right angled corners or parallel surfaces.

It's hard building decent walls with wonky stone, but if you look at old walls you see the trick – they used vast quantities of rough lime mortar packed out with gravel and small stones. Us ruffians with plenty of free stone try to economise on expensive mortar by fitting the stones more carefully, but the results are not usually very pretty. Climbing plants, trailing plants and moss eventually make them look OK though.

If you are fortunate enough to live somewhere the local stone breaks cleanly into regular slabs with parallel surfaces, or rich enough to buy in posh stone, I guess you treat it like brickwork. I've never been that lucky.

Blocks

The only blocks worth using in the garden are concrete. 'Breeze' blocks, the very light insulating type, are only suitable for indoor use or for the inside skin of a cavity wall. Blockwork is quick and cheap, but also grey and ugly. It can be rendered and painted, though.

Concrete blocks are designed to work with bricks so typically they are two bricks long and three bricks high. That makes for fast building, but they are heavy and rough to handle. Blocks can be solid or hollow and either the same width as a single brick or double that for solid walls.

Hollow blocks are usually filled with concrete after laying. For retaining walls it is normal to put reinforcing rods through the hollow before pouring the concrete.

An interesting variant is 'mortarless' blocks that slot together before filling with concrete. These are gaining acceptance in real building but are overkill for a garden wall. A cheaper alternative is to use plain hollow blocks without mortar. With reinforcing rods into the foundation and filled with concrete, they don't really need mortar between the blocks.

Mortar

See pages 19-10 For detailed mixes see table on page 108

FOUNDATIONS

If the bottom of the wall isn't secure it will lean, crack or fall over. Maybe even all three in quick succession. That said, garden walls rarely need the sort of foundations used for buildings, unless you are building a retaining wall to hold up a serious amount of earth.

Getting a level foundation is essential.

For brick, block and regular stone the normal foundation is concrete poured into a trench a bit wider than the wall. How deep depends on the nature of the soil and the height of the wall. If you have firm subsoil near the surface then about 300mm into that will be fine for most purposes, but if you have deep soft topsoil and are building a high wall it might be wise to go a bit deeper. Building in N. Wales I usually find bedrock about 100-200mm down, so I just clear the loose stuff and pour concrete onto that.

The concrete slab on this terrace is easily strong enough to support a small garden wall, but it slopes a little for drainage. In order to start the brick work level it needed a wedge of cement casting on it first. To get a good grip I chipped the surface with a cold chisel and hammer, then rigged up some simple shuttering from tapered pieces of wood. Wet the surface slightly and trowel in a mortar made from four parts concreting (sharp) sand and one part cement.

If you are building low walls that don't have to support any great load and the ground is firm you can dispense with the concrete. Make sure the base of the trench is flat and build with concrete bricks/blocks or engineering bricks. Ordinary commons don't last long underground.

Engineering bricks make a good foundation.

Most of this wall rests on concrete, but the end section where it disappears into the hill side just rests on Rhiwabon red bricks firmly seated by pounding them down with the end of a scaffold board.

Foundations for a new retaining wall - before the old one collapses!

For rough stone walls I've evolved a better method. Sort out a few large stones with at least one decent flat surface. Half fill the trench with concrete and stand the stones in it, taking care to get the best sides facing out, standing up straight and lined up with a board or a piece of taught string. Shovel the rest of the concrete around them, leaving about half of each stone sticking out.

If it's a retaining wall, one row of stones

on the front are all you need, but if it's a normal wall where both sides are going to be visible, put in two rows and make sure they are parallel and the right distance apart. Building with rough stones isn't easy, but it is slightly easier if you have something to work from.

If you have some big stones, you can avoid the concrete, and the trench doesn't even have to be flat. Just start with some big stones firmly bedded in the subsoil. That's how our house was built 200 years ago, and it hasn't fallen down yet.

Techniques

If you get the chance, watch an expert. If the expert is friendly, ask questions. Failing that, build something unimportant where few will see it!

Bricks and blocks are treated much the same. Lay down a bed of mortar on the foundation.

A mortar bed ready for the next course.

Plonk a brick on it and tap it down. Check it's level. Wipe the excess mortar from the faces with your trowel.

'Butter' the end of the next brick and butt it against the first. Tap it sideways to make a good joint and it will tend to settle down due to gravity. Sometimes you need to tap it on top too. Blocks are too heavy to hold one-handed while you 'butter' them, so put the mortar on the vertical end of a block after laying it, ready for the next one to butt up to.

Check the two bricks are level before you carry on.

On subsequent courses (rows) check that the side of the wall and the end is upright.

If you are building a 9" wall, put a small amount of mortar between the rows (Stretchers), but not much because you need to put some courses across the wall (called Headers) to bind it together and the width is determined by the length of the bricks you lay across. It's not a bad idea therefore to start with a course of headers so you have something to line up the next course with.

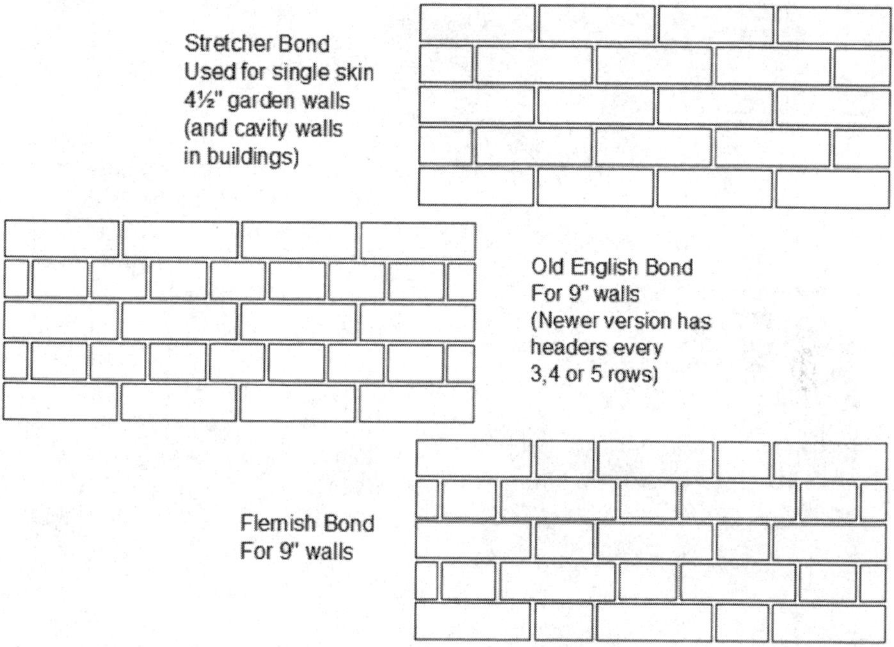

"Three common bricklaying bonds"

Look at old walls in your area. They vary a lot but it is common to put headers after every three to five courses of stretchers. 'Old English' bond alternates courses of headers and stretchers and 'Flemish' alternates headers and stretchers on every course, fiddly at corners or ends because you need quarter bricks, but it looks good done with old bricks.

Mix'n'Match

Building with a mixture of bricks can be a challenge. Here we have some rather skinny commons teamed up with some moulded facing bricks. To keep each course level takes a lot of mortar between the commons and almost none between the facing bricks.

Matching different size bricks with LOTS of mortar.

The object here was to make good use of a stash of weird shaped bricks and economise on the commons by reducing the wall thickness in the middle. It posed some problems. The facing bricks are much thicker than the commons, and longer too, which causes problems when using them as headers. Luckily the back of the wall will be hidden by a shed.

Overhanging course supported until the mortar hardens.

On the course above the 'picture frame' I thought the shaped end would be lighter, so they'd stay put until the cement hardened. They don't because the width of the commons on the course beneath is less than half a brick's length. Hence the Heath Robinson prop to hold them level. Once the cement hardens and the 'picture' is cement rendered they will be quite firm.

Archery

Building arches is fun. Cheaper than buying a lintel too. You need a former to support the arch while you build it. In this case I had already assembled the door, so rather than try to

If you already have the door, use it.

Unless the arch is half round you will need an angled spring point.

Guess I was lucky.

duplicate the shape I just fixed a piece of 6mm MDF over the top. If I'd had any sense I would have done the same down the sides of the door and built the walls up to it – they'd have been straighter then!

Arches can be half round, pointy like a gothic church or quite flat as shown here. This one only rises about 200mm across a 900mm width. I'm not sure I'd like to build flatter than that.

Flattish arches like this need a weird shaped brick to 'spring' from. If you have an angle grinder you can cut one. If not then cut some wood (as shown) and fill in behind the brick with a strong cement/sharp sand mortar. Let it harden a while before you build the rest.

Build your arch from both sides. If you are very lucky or very good at geometry, an equal number of bricks each side will either meet in the middle or leave exactly enough space for a final one to slot into the top. In the real world you might not be that lucky. If the gap is only slightly less than a brick's thickness you can carve a side off a brick with a cold chisel. If the gap is very small a terracotta tile or two will finish it off nicely.

You can't build a decent arch with random stone but if you haven't got any decent stone to use, old brick teamed with rough stone looks OK.

BRICK TIES

Bonding patterns are used on solid walls, but with the development of cavity walls in building work, some means of holding the two leaves parallel was needed. In the nineteenth century in Lancashire they built terraced houses with wooden lath ties and in the 20th century when we owned one, all the wood had rotted and it was quite common for the front to fall off a house in the night. Maybe this is why in many other regions solid walls were built well into the 1930s! Since then builders have used galvanised wire ties (butterfly ties) across cavities.

You aren't likely to need a cavity wall in a garden, but you can use the ties to join a wall to an existing one. To do this you need to hack out the mortar in the existing wall and grout in ties as you build the new one adjoining it. It's not easy, and unless you go deep into the old wall it's not a very good joint either.

Better are these screw in ties. There are many designs often sold as 'frame ties' because you can screw them into door and widow frames and embed them into the wall as you build.

Screw-in 'frame ties' are good on wonky old walls.

To fix to an old wall, just drill and rawlplug. To get the height right rest a brick, without mortar, on the wall you've built so far and mark as shown in the photo. The body of a chunky marker compensates for the lack of mortar.

Mark the height, drill and rawlplug for your tie.

Alligator ties fit into a rail that is screwed to the wall.

The ties just slot in with a quarter twist action.

Note the paint and loose mortar hacked from the old wall to help the mortar get a grip. Remove the brick to give you room to work, and drill into the old wall. Fit the tie and carry on building. One tie every 3-4 courses is sufficient.

Alligator ties are even stronger, but only suitable for good brick or concrete walls. You rawlplug the backing plate to the existing wall then drop in a tie every few courses.

Butterfly ties are useful if you want to build a wall at a weird angle. Unless you have a large angle grinder or 'Stihl Saw' you cannot do conventional brick bonds at anything but 90° or 180°. Even if you do cut bricks to odd angles, the cut faces will look strange, so it's better to butt joint them so the cuts are hidden inside the wall, and add butterflies for strength.

Work out where the corner is going to be and work from there, otherwise you may reach the corner and realise you need a tiny piece to make the length. See the drawing for a tip on making neat corners.

WITHOUT TIES (Cut edges visible)

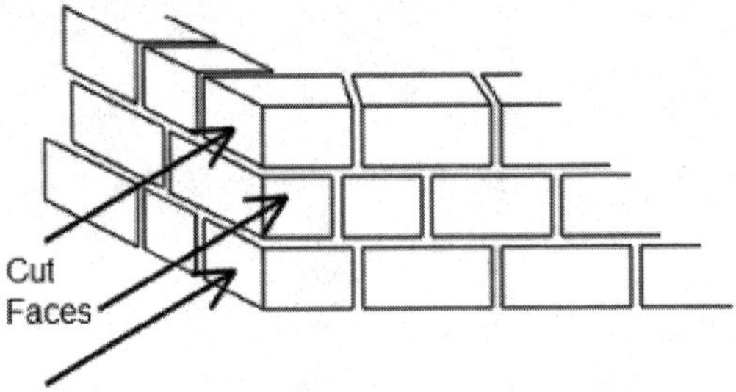

WITH TIES (Cut edges hidden)

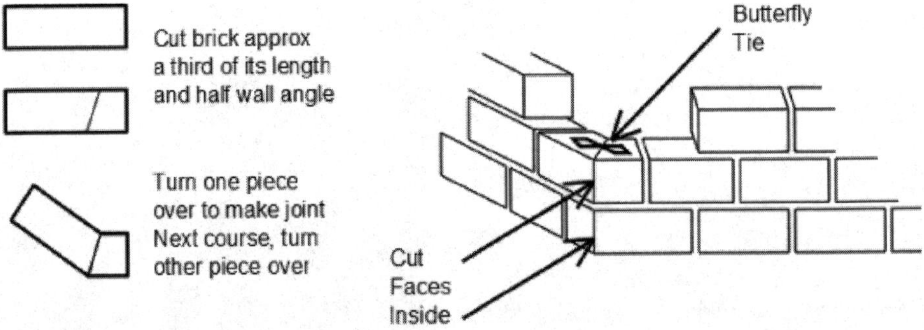

RENDERING

Rendering is nearly as much 'fun' as plastering indoors. There's a fine line between success and having the render all round your feet. If the mix is too wet it slides down the wall and if it is too dry it doesn't stick. If you work it too much, the moisture disappears and the render falls off. If it's too thick its weight pulls it off. Between 6-10mm is about right.

Scratch the first layer to help the finish get a grip.

The finished render, nothing a bit of filler and paint won't hide.

Tackle a small area first. It's surprisingly hard work and you need practice before you tackle a walled garden! Render is applied in two layers, using slightly different mixes (see page 108 for suitable rendering mixes), the first optimised for sticking to bricks, the second for sticking to the first and giving you a good finish. It's tempting to economise on the cement and/or lime but don't, that would make it even less likely to stick to the wall.

If you are rendering over common bricks, wet them first. If you don't they will suck water from the render and it will fall off. This isn't a problem with facing bricks, but if they are smooth and shiny the render won't grip. You need to rough them up a bit. Scoring with an angle grinder will do it.

Slap the first coat on without trying too hard to get it smooth, then flatten it by 'strickling' with the edge of a board. Hold the board level and move it side to side while gradually working it down the wall. Repeat this holding the board upright and working it across. This will take off any bumps and reveal the hollows, which you can fill if they are really bad. Don't fiddle too much. Score the surface into a diamond pattern with the edge of your float to help the next coat get a grip. Then leave it for a day or two.

Apply the second coat in the same manner. Hopefully this time you'll be more experienced and find it easier to get it flat.

STONE WALLS

Ruffian stone wall at the front to match the old one at the back.

Building in stone requires a different frame of mind, you don't think in courses. In fact you get a stronger wall by deliberately mixing small and large stones. 'Rubble' walls are the most common type for ruffians, basically two outer skins of your best stone with the middle filled with small stone, old dried up mortar, gravel, brick-bats and anything else you want to get rid of. It is a good idea to sling in some mortar from time to time, and add a few long stones across the wall like 'headers' in a brick wall.

Start with a few big stones lined up with a plank or taut string, then fill in the gaps (see foundations, pages 26-28), but don't aim to build a level course. Before you've reached the tops of the first big stones, sort out some more big'uns and set them carefully between the first lot using a plank or string as before to get them straight. Then fill in between them too. Providing you check the alignment each time you put in the major stones you can do the rest by eye.

Don't forget rubble walls need good capping to keep the rain out. At the very least save some good flat stones for the top and make sure they are well mortared in place.

CONCRETE FENCING/WALLING

Developers often divide up suburban housing estates with wooden fence panels slotted into concrete posts. To prevent the wood resting on the ground and rotting, the old method was to dig a trench and fill it with gravel that would drain and keep the fence dry. The modern method is to use concrete panels, often known as 'gravel boards' since they serve the same function of keeping the wooden panels off the ground.

The reason I mention this here rather than in 'Fencing' is that the 'gravel boards' can be used to make a simple wall. Fencing is another great British metrication disaster. The panels are made in feet and the posts in metric! Gravel boards are usually 6' x 1', so you can make a 3' retaining wall like this by using 1.5M posts set into concrete almost 2' deep for stability.

I accept gravel boards are not to everyone's taste, but if you don't like the look they might still have a use like here where the retaining wall will form part of a shed wall and not be visible.

Concrete panels make a sturdy retaining wall.

If you want an old rustic dry stone wall appearance but need to hold up an embankment, use concrete fencing then build your stone wall in front of it.

PAINTING

Painting is a great way of unifying disparate materials. This terrace is bounded by an old stone cottage, a concrete retaining wall and a brick wall built from salvaged bricks in three different colours. By painting all the walls white, using the same colour on the gate and the shutters and painting the panel to match another wall panel you can't see in this shot, the whole area looks like it was designed.

The long term plan is for Linda to paint a mural in the panel, but by the time I'd finished the wall it was bit late in the year for al fresco artwork. The photo overleaf has been digitally altered to show how it will look – eventually!

Wish I'd digitally altered the floor too!

Masonry paint is obviously designed for the job, but you can use good quality emulsion paint outdoors. If the wall is new it's worth using a stabilising primer to counter the alkalinity of the mortar/render/concrete. It's useful on old walls that have previously been lime-washed too. One coat of primer and two of masonry paint should give a surface that will last ten years or so.

GABIONS

Gabions are wire baskets that are filled with rubble to reinforce embankments. You see them alongside motorway cuttings, railways, river banks – and in extreme gardens. There are two varieties; those made with a woven mesh like heavy-duty wire netting, or with 'weld-mesh' which looks like a lighter version of the stuff used to reinforce concrete. Both come in a range of sizes and are delivered 'flat packed' so you need to erect them, and you will need some strong galvanised wire to lash them together to make a wall.

Then you need a lot of stone and energy. Professionals will, of course, buy stone from a quarry, have it delivered by truck and shovel it in with a JCB. Ruffians like me, faced with an unstable bank, do it like this:

Now fill it with the rock you just dug out!

Buy a pick. Dig into the bank until you reach firm rock. Then dig some more until you have a vertical face and a flat bottom. Then dig even more until the flat bottom is a metre wide. Finally put a gabion in place and fill it with the stuff you just dug out. Put the decent size stones at the front and sides and shovel the rubble and soil in behind them. A 2 x 1 x 1 metre gabion takes about three tonnes of fill.

Gabions don't look all that great, though they do provide a good support for climbing plants. We converted a gabion wall to a concrete wall by erecting shuttering about 50mm in front of the gabions and pouring concrete into the gap. It would have been better if the concrete had been runnier though. Despite me ramming it down with the end of a board and banging the shuttering with a sledgehammer to help it settle, the surface isn't really very good.

CHAPTER 4

HARD SURFACES

Path, parking or patio; most of us need some hard surfaces. In our case, having hacked a path through the weeds to the back door and discovered a flattish area at the side of the house – it only slopes 0.6 of a metre in 5 metres – it seemed like a good place for a patio. Somewhere to hang washing, chop firewood and drink coffee.

It's rough and it slopes, but it's a nice place to sit.

That patio provided the inspiration for this book. Back then Ground Force was on the TV and in the bookshops, and Linda started to to give me advice from the words of Tommy Walsh: "Start by removing 5" of topsoil." It's not bad advice, either. He went on to explain that bricks are about 3" thick and you should lay them on 2" of sand, but the bedrock was visible at the top of our patio area and the lower end was mostly cinders. Topsoil? Hah!

STYLES, MATERIALS, TECHNIQUES AND ENVIRONMENT

I'm not trying to teach you style. I'm not the stylish type. Some materials, grey concrete slabs for example, look pretty dull, but in the right urban environment and contrasted with brighter surfaces they could be perfect. My only tip is, don't use too many different materials in the same area as it looks messy.

Where a lack of both cash and availability of cheap recycled materials means you have to use different materials, find some way of separating them, or unifying them. A brick path that suddenly turns into a concrete path where you ran out of bricks looks bad. A brick path that leads to steps or a gate looks better, even if after the steps/gate the rest of the path is concrete.

There are two important environmental concerns. Making cement is a very energy intensive business, but reusing concrete slabs and paviors helps reduce the overall energy use. Secondly, hard surfaces shed water too quickly. When rain falls on vegetation it soaks into the soil, replenishing the water table. When it falls on concrete it runs off into drains and water courses causing flash flooding followed by drought. Planning laws require porous paving on new developments and in an ideal world we'd all use it in our own projects. Unfortunately some of it is quite expensive. Cheap alternatives are gravel or crazy paving with gravel or grass between the stones, crushed slate – or a lawn. The rest of this chapter is about the really hard stuff. The softer surfaces come later.

Concrete Slabs

'Council' slabs for pavements are usually 2' x 3', but they are very heavy to handle and look a bit daft paving a small area. 2' x 2' are lighter and look better in most places and 18" are better still for small areas but more likely to become uneven if you drive on them. They don't have to be grey either. So called 'reconstituted stone' is just posh concrete and comes in all sorts of colours with more or less convincing textures.

Bricks

I mentioned bricks in the wall building section. Experts will tell you that ordinary common bricks are not suitable for paving since they are not frost proof. Actually many of them are quite durable and if some crumble after a few years they add to the rustic charm. When they stop being charming and become an unsightly hazard you have the job of prising the broken bits out and replacing them.

Frost damaged bricks can look attractive.

If you want a long lasting surface, buy concrete paviors. If money is no problem, buy recycled paving bricks or tiles. If you're a cheapskate like me, wait until you find a supply of old bricks going free and use those, whatever they are.

Stone

Traditional paving stones are rare and expensive. If you are lucky enough to have some, perhaps from relaying an old stone floor, don't smash them up for hardcore. If you don't want them, Freecycle them or sell them. If you want to use them, then the technique is much the same as for concrete slabs.

Pebbles set in concrete and surrounded by gravel.

Pebbles are cheaper – providing you can find some legally. It is illegal to remove pebbles (or sand) from a beach or river bed without permission from the Environment Agency. That said, if your property runs down to a beach, or to a rocky stream, removing a few by hand isn't going to cause an environmental disaster. Use some common sense and don't turn up with a digger and tipper truck!

Random Stone is OK for rustic paths, if you are excavating or demolishing, put all the stones with at least one decent surface to one side until you need another path. See the picture on page 22

Poured Concrete

It isn't pretty, and we've noted the environmental concerns, but there are times when a poured slab of concrete is the best solution. It's cheap, it's solid, it lasts a long time and it resists weeds. It's grey and boring and dusty too, but you can improve it with floor paint. (See page 37 Chapter 3)

Foundations

If you want the surface of your path/patio flat, you will need something underneath the bricks, stones or whatever that will give a little when you tap them down. For bricks or slabs that fit tightly together, coarse (concreting) sand is ideal. Pebbles and bits of random stone can be laid in mortar. For a very rustic effect you can bed large stone slabs (slate works well round these parts) into the soil and plant low growing plants like thyme and camomile (or grass) between them.

The sub surface is important too. You might not be able to 'remove 5" of topsoil', but you do need to make an effort to get the area flat (or nicely graded if a slope) and remove things like tree stumps and roots. Even a 'flat' area needs a slight slope towards a drain to stop puddles appearing.

A brick on edge gives a guide to the depth needed.

Weed growth is always an issue with anything other than a poured slab. You can prevent old weeds reappearing by laying some form of membrane on the soil before the sand goes down. Garden centres sell stuff specially for this, but you can also use old 'tarpaulins' and even cut up 'tonne' bags for paths.

For slabs or bricks lay 3-5cm (an inch or two) of coarse sand and rake it smooth.

Membrane, sand and a simple levelling guide.

For pebbles or random stone lay about the same depth of 'dry mix' ie. mortar without the water in it. But don't do a bigger area that you can cover in stones in one session or you'll have to dig it up again.

Tips, Techniques and Tools

For a really good 'grade' (slope) lay a couple of pieces of wood on the soil and level them. Put sand/mortar between them and 'strickle' it by resting another board across them and dragging it across the sand.

A rubber hammer is useful for whacking bricks down without cracking them. If you don't have one a wooden mallet will do (but you'll wreck it). Or use a piece of softwood on top of the brick and whack it with an ordinary hammer.

Have a long piece of straight wood handy to check the level of a long run of bricks, it's easy to lay two bricks next to each other so they look right, then discover 20 bricks down the line you've created a slope or a curve. If you are aiming for 'flat', use a spirit level on top of a plank rather than straight on the bricks; you'll get a better reading of how a long section of bricks are lying.

To provide a slight slope for drainage use a thin piece of wood between the level and the plank, 10 or 12mm (about ½") under one end of a 600mm level is about right.

If you are laying on sand, brush some more sand into the cracks to finish the job.

If you lay pebbles in dry mix, bed them about halfway in or slightly more. If the ground is wet the cement will absorb enough water to harden over a few days. If it looks like staying dry, water it lightly using a fine rose on a watering can. Bedding pebbles in wet mortar is much messier and it will be years before the pebbles look clean!

Edges

Heavy slabs don't need edges to help them stay in place, though you may want them for aesthetic reasons. Bricks and paviors do need them. Without firm edging the bricks will gradually drift further and further apart as grit and weeds insinuate themselves into the gaps. You can buy edging strip that peg into the ground but the ruffian method is a strip of concrete poured behind the outer line of bricks and just below the adjacent groundlevel so you can't see it.

Tilted bricks make a good edging.

Some change of pattern is traditional at the edge of paving and 'header' bricks on edge work well. Where the paving adjoins a plant bed with a raised soil level, putting bricks on end gives a 'kerbstone' effect. Tilting them is an old-fashioned technique that works well in cottage gardens.

Rough & Ready

You can take liberties with paths that don't get a lot of use. The example in the photo is only for the gardener to access the bank above and not a design feature. With very little traffic and plenty of pressure on the edging from the bank behind it, I didn't bother concreting behind the bricks.

My parents had brick paths in their cottage garden when I was a kid. They were laid straight onto the soil. When the weed growth got too bad my mum used to lift the bricks with a spade, dig out the weeds then put the bricks down again.

Steps

Steps aren't really a separate topic, they are just a series of low walls tapped by short paths! The surfaces need to be secure though, pretty well flat and not too slippery. Here's a few types that are easy to build:

- Simple brick steps, each step two bricks high topped off with a layer of mortar trowelled flat. Not very attractive but OK here where they connect the backyard to the lane.

- Similar brick construction but with slate steps. We discovered these in a bad state and repaired some, rebuilt others. In this case each new 'riser' is built on the edge of the previous step, making them quite steep. You can apply the same idea to any kind of stone/concrete slab.

- Just bricks. Two courses of bricks with no slab is a bit low for most steps, three is a bit steep. One normal course with the step surface made from bricks on edge works out about right. (If you're wondering why there's a step in front of a wall, it works like a stile; there's another one round the other side.)

- Providing the soil is firm and not given to landslides you can build brick steps without foundations or mortar too. Cut into the bank with a spade, disturbing the soil as little as possible, and bang the bricks down firmly. Rough and ready steps won't last forever, but they'll get you up and down a treacherous bank for a few years.

It's a brick stile.

Stone and concrete steps are rough but solid.

- Stone and Concrete. The risers are random stone to match the walls, but on completion of each riser I put a board across the front and filled in behind with rough concrete (ie. concrete containing a lot of small stone left over from the wall building.

- Logs. In a wooded area what's more natural than logs? Actually some of these are treated, roughly rounded logs from a timber yard, others are just bits of a tree that was getting in the way. The previous logs lasted 10 years, then became a fungii and bug reserve. Fine for free.

Natural logs will last about 10 years.

Unless the logs are embedded in the bank at the sides, they need staking.

- You need some stakes to stop the logs rolling downhill. Branches off the same tree about 50mm in diameter and 500mm long are ideal, roughly pointed to help them go in. In stony ground it helps to drive a steel rod of some sort in first then wiggle it about a bit and pull it out to leave a pilot hole for the stake.

A sledgehammer is the ideal tool to bash them in with but if you don't have one then pounding them with a heavy log works too.

- Board and gravel. Just a variation on the logs really, but the boards are 'tanalized' and should last 20 years. The gravel helps stop them getting waterlogged. Once again you need to stake them, but probably in this case with tanalized posts.

Quick and easy steps with tanalized boards and gravel.

Cover slippery boards in chicken wire for grip.

- Wooden steps, made from tanalized timber or just old pallets. Either way, they get slippery with moss and mould so cover with chicken wire for a non-slip surface.

CONCRETE

There's no getting away from concrete. If you want a cheap(ish) and hard-wearing surface for a yard or a base for a shed, it's hard to beat.

For a yard that only gets walked on you can get away with about 50mm of concrete providing the base is firm. If you are going to drive on it or use it for chopping wood or something equally strenuous you'd better double that. Bases for a light shed should be somewhere between the two and for serious sheds, outdoor offices, workshops and the like, 100mm is good.

This means that for anything but a tiny yard you'll need a serious amount of concrete, and mixing it by hand is hard work. If it looks like you'll be laying concrete and building walls for some years, it's worth buying a mixer. Second-hand ones do crop up, but a new one isn't very expensive and if you look after it you can sell it once you've finished. If it's only a one-off job, hire one for a day.

Steel isn't normally necessary for a shed base, but here...

Flattening a concrete slab.

Finished slab with cantilevered floor extension.

It isn't absolutely essential to put a load of old bricks and rock under your concrete slab, but you do need a good solid surface and hardcore is cheap (or free if you live in a giant rockery like we do!). Whack it down firmly and roughly level.

If the ground is firm and you aren't planning to drive HGVs on your concrete you don't need any steel in it. However, the base for my office is laid on the side of a hill and has to support a cantilevered floor, so we used 100mm weld mesh in it.

You do need some form of shuttering around the area and '4 x 2' or '3 x 2' timber are fine for a shed base. Don't be tempted to use thinner boards though as they'll only bend. Whack stakes into the ground to hold the shuttering steady, and level the top surfaces. If the shuttering is right, you can use a board to tamp the surface down level, but if it isn't you'll struggle to get it flat.

To extend the floor out over the edge of the bank we laid four 1.5m concrete fence posts horizontally on the hardcore and laid the weld mesh over them. The shuttering was arranged so the posts stuck out 600mm and came 50mm higher than the posts. Then we poured concrete over the lot. Putting the posts 50mm below the slab surface means that 2" thick planks laid on the posts make a level floor. Obviously concrete posts are not intended for this and you have to use some common sense about how much they stick out and how much load you put on them. In this case the whole office is 3m wide with just 0.6m of it hanging over the edge.

Mix the sand, aggregate and cement dry first until it's well blended, then gradually add water. You want it runny enough to level easily, but not so wet it self-levels and water pools on the surface. See page 108 for mixes and quantities.

Tip the concrete in and level it roughly with a shovel. Now you will need a board long enough to reach right across the surface resting on the shuttering and two strong people to strickle it across the surface.

If you lift it a little, move it a little and then bang it down, and repeat and repeat this, you'll get a flat surface with ridges. This is fine for a shed base, and the ridged surface is ideal for building on, but if the surface is going to be visible you need to 'float' it smooth with a plasterer's steel float.

If it's a really big area, do it in slabs small enough to manage, possibly something like 3 x 4m if you are doing it by hand.

CHAPTER 5

SOFTER SURFACES

GRAVEL

Softer porous surfaces are great for allowing rainwater to replenish the water table rather than running straight into the nearest drain, but they do have to be chosen wisely. Conventional gravel, for instance, is associated with grand houses with long sweeping gravel drives and forecourts where the chauffeur can decant the rich and glamorous. What's not so glamorous is that every time you make a sweeping entrance, or hasty exit, you scatter gravel in all directions. Unless you have a gardener standing by with a rake to tidy up after every arrival or departure, maybe you should think of something else.

Gravel paths are OK here. No-one in heels can get up the steps!

Gravel isn't popular with women wearing heels either. It scuffs them, apparently. If you like the look of a broad sweep of gravel, but want something firmer to walk on, set 'stepping stones' amid the gravel.

CRUSHED SLATE

Crushed slate is an alternative, though rarely seen in North Wales despite there being plenty of slate heaps around. Maybe the association with its former use in factory yards and quarry roads puts people off. Bought in little bags in suburban garden centres, it isn't cheap, so I've experimented with slate waste from a local quarry. After bashing it with a hammer for hours to reduce the size, I hit on the idea of loading it into the cement mixer with some big rocks and a bucketful of water. After a lot of bashing and splashing, empty the mixer into a soil sieve. It wasn't a hugely successful operation by any means, though.

Gravel and slate both benefit from being laid on a weed resistant membrane, and both need decent edging to stop them migrating into the surrounding ground.

GRASS - LAWN

The lawn is the archetypal British solution to covering ground, and not a bad one in our climate. It absorbs water when it rains, yet can survive the occasional dry summer. If you have plenty of time and energy you can pamper it and produce something resembling green velvet, or with minimum work you can have somewhere for kids to play and adults to relax. I'm assuming if you're reading this you're interested in the latter type.

To produce a rough and ready lawn you need to remove all the rocks, tree stumps and deeply rooted perennial weeds and rake the soil flat. Walk all over it to firm it up and rake the surface again. Drag a board across it to show up where the lumps and bumps are, then flatten them and rake it some more. Now tread it again and repeat this process until you're happy, or exhausted.

Grass seed can be planted in spring or autumn (April or September usually) so start the preparation in plenty of time. Scatter it quite thinly as it'll spread when it grows.

Birds love grass seed, and cats appreciate the freshly raked earth too. You can make life difficult for them and reduce the damage a bit by pushing sticks into the ground and stretching pea-netting across the area until the seeds sprout.

Grass soon wears out if you walk on the same bit regularly. If a path is too much work or the grassy patch is too small to divide up, use stepping stones. Visually it's still one patch, but the wear is reduced considerably.

GRASS – ROUGH

If you have a large garden, leave some of it rough, at least until you have the rest of it under control. If you strim it 3-4 times a year it looks OK. The weeds in our garden (mostly hogweed) were taller taller than me when we moved in. After 10 years of regular strimming we now simply run a Flymo over parts of it in the summer to define a path to the fruit trees and bushes.

BARK

Serious gardeners often use composted bark as a mulch for plant beds. It helps to suppress weed growth and seeds that take root in it can be pulled out easily – provided you get to them before they've rooted in the underlying soil.

It makes a pretty good surface under climbing frames, swings and slides too – but the kids will kick it all over the garden. It works best if you dig a pit about 150-200mm deep and line it with a weed resistant membrane, then pile in the bark.

Tanalized timber edges suit the woodland look but if you want them darker use a garden stain or paint. 'Creocote' is a brand name preservative that looks a bit like creosote without the carcinogenic properties.

Make sure the pit is big though as there's no point providing a soft surface if your kids fly straight across it when they fall off the swing and crack their heads on the edging!

CHAPTER 6

WATER HARVESTING

Attitudes to water management around buildings have changed considerably over the years. When our cottage was built the norm was to dig several pits around it, fill them with rubble, run drains into them, top them off with bigger stones and replace the top soil. All the downspouts ran into 'soak-aways' like this so rain water was directed into the soil.

More recently Building Society surveyors have taken to having a fit of the vapours about this and write worrying reports about how the groundwater will destroy your foundations and insist that the downspouts run into proper drains. This isn't a great idea as it leads to the drainage system being overloaded when it rains, and well publicised instances of water companies dumping untreated sewage when systems cannot cope during downpours. Even when they can cope it means they are wasting resources processing extra water, which they then put into a river. Replenishing the water table in the ground is a much better idea.

Old soak-aways don't work as well as they used to though and eventually they become clogged with soil. Unless you fancy protracted negotiations with your mortgage provider followed by digging a new one to their spec, it might be easier to agree to conventional drainage, then divert as much water as possible into butts or tanks for garden use. If you are really smart you can re-plumb your house to use rainwater for toilet flushing and with minimum filtering for supplying a washing machine, but that's beyond the scope of this book.

BUTTS AND TANKS

Old wooden barrels look great beside olde-worlde cottages, but they don't come cheap. Plastic water butts from garden centres aren't that cheap either, but fortunately there is an alternative for the dedicated cheapskate – industrial plastic drums and tanks.

You do need to find a reputable supplier though, avoiding the dodgy geezer with a pile of drums in his backyard that once held dangerous chemicals. Food containers are good. I bought two 100 litre mango chutney drums from a car boot sale for £14 the pair. They were fly-blown and sticky but at least you know they are not poisonous. There are specialists all over the country selling a wide range of tanks and drums and many of them also sell fittings, taps and pipes. If you are in NW England or NE Wales try www.dvfuels.co.uk who will deliver, but carting empty drums around isn't cheap, so contact them for a quote. The larger tanks are more economical to transport. If transport from N Wales is too dear, get Googling.

Support

Unless you are installing pumps you need your water butt high enough to get a bucket or watering can under the tap, so it needs to stand on something, and that something has to be strong. 100 litres of water weighs 100kg (one reason I like metric, the sums are easier), so a flimsy wooden box isn't going to last long. Bricks are good, with or without mortar. We have one standing on a cast iron oven from an ancient fireplace.

Connections

The simplest connection is to arrange the downspout to run straight into the top of the butt, but there are a couple of issues – leaves and overflows.

Autumn leaves are notorious for blocking gutters, and in particular downpipes. If the top of the butt is open it will soon fill with leaves and other debris, so it helps if you keep the lid and make a hole just big enough for the pipe to enter.

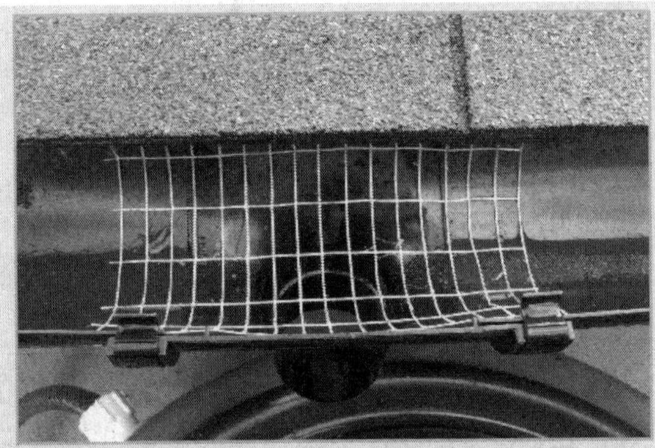

A bit of mesh keeps the leaves out.

If you have a short vertical pipe into a water butt, maybe it won't block, but you'll get decomposing leaves in the butt instead which don't smell too good, and in due course they'll clog the tap. Put some kind of mesh over the top of the downpipe to stop them. 'Chicken wire' scrunched into a ball and stuffed in the top of the pipe is good and a little off-cut of mesh from a pet cage or poultry run works well too.

If it rains a lot your butt will soon overflow. Rather than having the surplus water just run down the side and onto the floor, you should really organise an overflow system.

A WC cistern overflow pipe is ideal for water butts.

This one uses pipework sold for WC cistern overflows, running into a gulley that just happened to be in the right place.

If you need to get the overflow away from the house, a hosepipe works well enough. Fit a WC overflow fitting near the top of the butt. A reinforced hose will slide into it easily. To make a decent seal, pull some hose through into the butt, then wrap 'gaffer tape' (or duct tape or even Duck Tape, it's all the same stuff) round the end until it's just too fat to go back through the fitting, then pull it hard from the outside so it wedges. In this case the hose goes over a cliff onto waste ground but in more civilised gardens you might need to run it into a proper drain.

If you are really civilised you can buy automatic water butt connections from garden centres. These intercept water running down the walls of a downpipe and feed it into the butt. When the butt is full water runs back through the connector into the downpipe.

Hose is more convenient for longer runs.

Places that sell tanks and drums often sell taps as well. The cheap plastic taps designed for water butts can be a problem on drums.

They are designed to fit to flattish surfaces, so if you buy a square tank they are OK and if you buy a proper water butt it will have a flat section for the tap, but if you buy a cylindrical drum it won't. You can bodge the tap with lots of PTFE tape but you won't get a good seal and it will keep working loose and leaking. If you try to get the thing really tight, you'll just damage the plastic screw thread.

Brass fittings are a much better bet and they come with substantial nuts with a wide flange so you can get them really tight and they'll flatten the plastic to make a decent seal.

A brass tap suitable for a water butt. (photo courtesy of Crocus)

For more elaborate plumbing, recent developments in push-fit fittings are a real boon. Using brass tank fittings, 15mm copper pipe and plastic push-fit fittings you can easily link together several water butts or large tanks, and pipe the water to a convenient place in the garden – providing it is lower than the water butts. Link the butts near the bottom, and take a branch off the link to your tap(s). The level will be the same in all of them, so you only need one overflow.

Butts linked with push-fit plumbing.

This setup is practical, tidy and just a bit sentimental for me. The mango chutney drums are on the 'scruffy side' of our back yard wall where they collect rain off the back of the house and a woodshed. The water is piped through the wall to an old brass tap on the prettier side of the wall.

Two butts are better than one.

That tap has a history. It was the only tap in the cottage where I was born until when I was a teenager my dad and I fitted a 'modern' kitchen with a chrome tap and a water heater. After my dad died I cleared out his shed and found it. It was probably installed in the 1930s when an old farmhouse and adjoining barn were converted into three cottages, but knowing our landlord it was probably second-hand even then.

I have thought about fitting electric pumps to our water butts to lift surplus water to a larger tank at the top of the garden to harvest water for household use, but the thought of the work involved, and keeping it working and ice-free in the winter, puts me off.

GUTTERING

I'm assuming you are just collecting water from existing down pipes, but if you are building an extension, shed or greenhouse you will need to fit guttering. To keep the water moving it needs a slight slope, but only about 6-10mm per metre.

If you have a stand-alone shed with guttering on two sides, two downpipes and two water butts would be a bit over the top. A cheaper, easier alternative is to run a continuous gutter along both sides and across one end. It might take a bit more wood work and guttering, but you will save on butts and taps.

Alternatively, place the butt at the end of the shed, and run the downpipes diagonally into it from each side.

One gutter collects water from both sides.

MAKING HOLES

To plumb a water butt you need to make some big holes in it, and bigger than the drills most of us own too. 'Chain drilling' is the answer. Draw the hole with a felt tip (the permanent type work well on plastic), then use a small (3-4mm) drill in a power drill to make a series of holes close together just inside the line.

Now you have a choice. You can either cut between the holes with a small sharp chisel or carefully drag the drill bit sideways to cut from hole to hole. This is a bit tricky and if you are not careful the drill will break, or go off course. Finish off the hole with a file, a round one for small holes or the curved side of a half-round for larger ones. Make the hole as accurate as possible to ensure a leak-proof job.

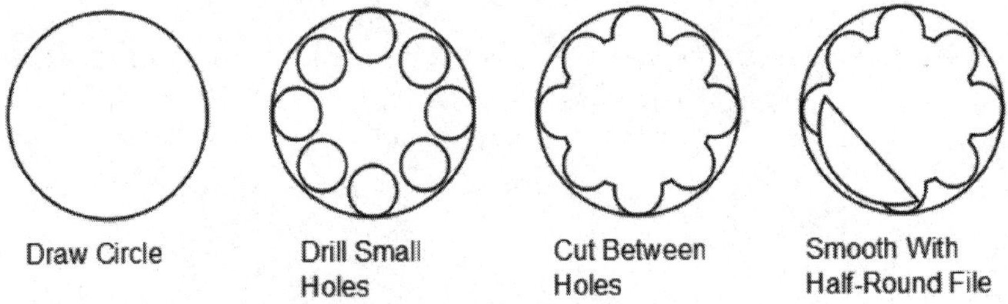

Chain drilling a large hole in a water butt.

CHAPTER 7

REPAIR AND REUSE

Re-cycling materials gets a lot of attention and obviously it makes more sense than burying stuff in holes in the ground. Reusing things makes even more sense since the transport and processing costs are next to zero. I've already mentioned second-hand bricks, industrial drums for water butts, chimney pots and assorted cans for for planters, but there are plenty more things you can reuse.

You don't have to limit yourself to reusing your own junk either. If you join the Freecycle network (www.uk.freecycle.org) you can get rid of stuff you really have no use for, and relieve other members of things you can use. There are local recycling groups on Yahoo too. Failing that, car boot sales, garage/yard sales, charity shops, markets and jumble sales are all cheap.

Here's a round up of reused stuff in our garden.

Greenhouse

A new base for an old greenhouse.

Many people buy greenhouses in a fit of enthusiasm, then get rid of them when they realise they aren't growing anything. They appear on Freecycle occasionally. The one on page 6 came from a friend's garden, but she got it second-hand from somewhere. It took a while to dismantle it and re-erect it, and it needed quite a lot of new glass and new glazing clips to hold in the glass, but these items are readily available from hardware stores.

It's fixed to four 8" x 4" pressure treated planks and floored with old bricks laid on recycled dumpy bags and sand.

Shed

You sometimes find sheds on Freecycle, the deal usually being that you have to dismantle it and remove it, often against a tight deadline because the owner is selling up, moving or getting the garden made over. Failing that you might build one, but before you rush out and buy stuff, its worth seeing what you can scrounge.

New shed using recycled materials.

This shed has doors from Freecycle and the planking to the left of the doors is from pallets. The back walls are old shuttering ply from a concrete project, but a few more pallets would have done as well; it just depends what you have or can get hold of. Unfortunately the frame and the roof are made from new timber.

Office

Most of this office is new, but the French windows came from a friend's house and the other windows from a builder who was putting an extension on a house nearby and taking out the old windows. They are double glazed and had been in situ less than 10 years.

A lot of recycling went into this office.

Under the floor is 'Kingspan' foam from www.secondsandco.co.uk but it's not actually second-hand, it's slightly substandard and/or damaged. I guess some of it has been damaged in transit or on site and rejected by builders. It works fine under the floor though. Seconds and Co also sell loft insulation, which went into the walls.

The light fittings and stove were second-hand too. All it took was a couple of hours to clean up the stove with a wire brush and apply a coat of stove paint, and now it keeps me warm while I write.

Even the furniture is stuff we chucked out of the house, and the computers (currently three) are either second-hand or assembled from components bought on Ebay.

Bench

We bought this new in a sale at a well known DIY store. The wooden slats were rubbish and not pressure treated and given only a thin coat of indoor quality varnish. Consequently it started to fall apart after two winters. The ends are cast aluminium though and will last years, so I bought some pressure-treated 2" x 1" and a bag of screws and re-built it.

Better than new with new slats fitted.

Gate

The gate next to the bench above is the top surface of a pallet, one of the rare ones with a close-boarded surface. If you can't get one, take a conventional 'gappy' pallet and nail a few more boards in between the existing ones.

Sharpening is easier with a jig.

TOOLS

Car boot sales often have garage clearances, with guys selling a lifelong accumulation of stuff that might have come in useful, but never did. That often includes old tools, some broken and some just in need of a clean up.

Finally, invest in a wire brush, some emery cloth and oil to polish iron and steel.

If you pick up woodworking tools you'll need an oil stone for sharpening chisels and plane irons, and if you are not used to using them a sharpening jig is useful. This holds the blade at the correct angle while you rub it up and down the stone, and it comes with an instruction leaflet.

Garden tools such as hoes and spades work better if they are sharp and you will need a file for that. Files you find in sales are usually old and rusty and not worth having. If you find a new one though, they often come without handles. Hardware stores used to sell file handles but many now sell DIY grade files with moulded plastic handles. Sometimes it's worth making a silly offer for old files just to knock the handles off and re-use them.

Saws with replaceable blades such as hacksaws, coping saws and bow (log) saws are generally good value and with a replacement blade they are as good as new. Hand (woodworking) saws are not so great. Sharpening them and 'setting' the teeth is a skilled trade and time consuming. If the blade is rusty it will never work well. Newer saws have very hard teeth that last quite a long time, but once blunt they really are useless and you cannot sharpen them since the teeth are as hard as a saw file.

Hammer heads last for ever and handles are cheap.

This hammer came from an even cheaper source. I literally dug it up in the garden. It didn't have a handle at the time but new handles are cheaper than new hammers.

The cold chisel turned up in a garage clear-out. Cold chisels get a mushroom effect from repeated striking and eventually pieces will fly off. This can be extremely dangerous, so if you get an old one you need to grind the end flat, and slightly chamfered at the edge.

This shovel was also from a clear-out and hasn't got a new handle yet, but it will one day. To remove the remains of the old handle, stick it in a stove, open

New handle needed.

fireplace or bonfire. Once the wood is charred you can knock the remains out. Don't let the blade get too hot though, or you'll soften it. And don't quench the hot socket end in water as it will make it brittle. Just let it cool down naturally.

A portable workbench is very useful if you are doing fencing, making a gate or any kind of woodwork outdoors. Once again they crop up on Freecycle, or in car boots. The top surface of the best ones is very thick good quality plywood, but cheaper ones are MDF or chipboard. All of them get cut up by ham-fisted users and all are susceptible to decay or de-lamination if left out in the rain. Fortunately, replacing the top isn't hard, and can be almost free if you use pallet wood. See the next chapter for a detailed guide.

WOOD

There ought to be a law against throwing wood away. It grieves me to see it in builders' skips mixed in with plasterboard and rubble because I know it's just going to go into landfill. Never, ever throw wood away.

Off-cuts and leftovers will come in useful eventually. Sound timber salvaged from demolition or re-building in the house can be fashioned into fencing, gates or shuttering for concrete; the list is endless. Really small off-cuts and rotten timber I chop up for firewood.

I make an exception for second-hand chipboard as there is no use for it outdoors and if you leave it outside for long it will treble its weight with the amount of water it absorbs. Then it starts to fall apart and smell. It doesn't burn well in woodburning stoves either, but it isn't bad in stoves with open grates for solid fuel.

Pallets are a great source of free wood. So good Joe Jacobs has written a whole book about them (available from The Good Life Press). Many companies that buy materials in bulk have them delivered on pallets and soon have a heap of them getting in the way. A bit of sweet talking and they are often yours for the taking.

CHAPTER 8

WOODWORK (NO WORKSHOP)

If you are a keen woodworker with thousands of pounds worth of tools and machinery in a heated workshop, this chapter will make you ill. If you have a handful of basic tools and nowhere flat enough to build a workshop even if you could afford one, this is for you. If you don't even have the basic tools, see Chapter 10 for advice. You really don't need to spend a fortune.

PRINCIPLES

All traditional woodwork is the way it is because wood has a grain. Trees have evolved with hollow fibrous structures to carry water (and trace minerals) up to the leaves and sugar created in the leaves back down to the growing outer layer of wood. They can wriggle about a bit but basically those fibres run up and down the trunk of the tree and show up as lines running along the length of a plank.

FROM TREE TO WOOD

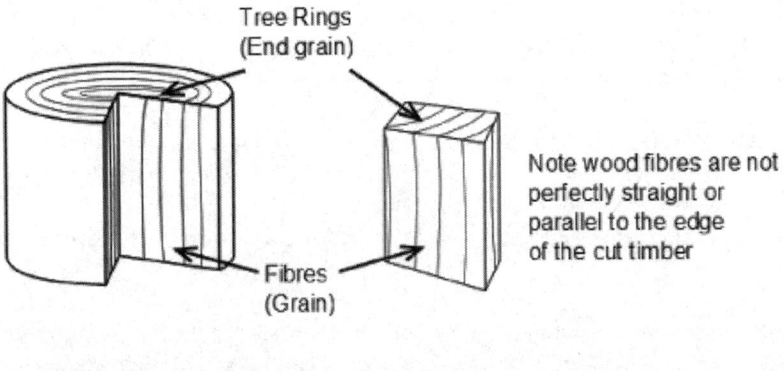

The fibres in a piece of wood are strong, but the connection between them is much less so. Wood is hard to break across the grain, but often splits along the grain as the fibres separate. This affects the way you work it and explains why some bits of wood plane nice and smoothly one way, but cut up rough when you turn them round. Look at the grain closely and you'll see that it doesn't run quite parallel to the surface and planing in the wrong direction is like stroking a cat backwards. Some types of wood have very twisty grain patterns which makes them hard to work but less likely to split. They can be pretty too if you do manage to get them smooth.

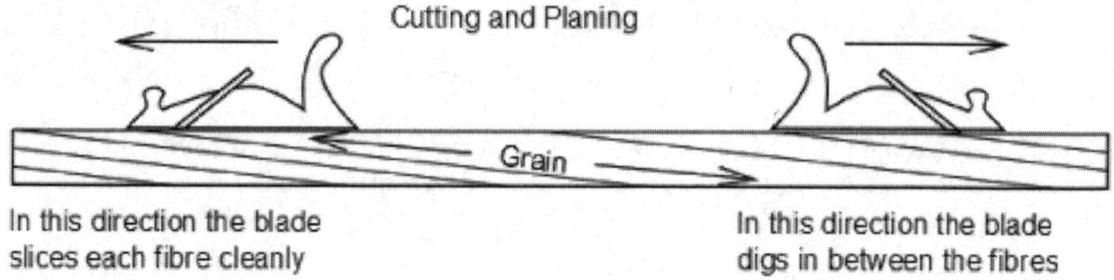

Grain has several other consequences for woodwork too. When the tree was growing the fibres were full of water. Trees are usually cut during the autumn/ winter when they are drier, but even so there is a lot of water in them. As the water dries out the fibres shrink. If an entire log is dried it will develop splits and if a log is cut into planks and boards they will warp as the fibres contract. If you

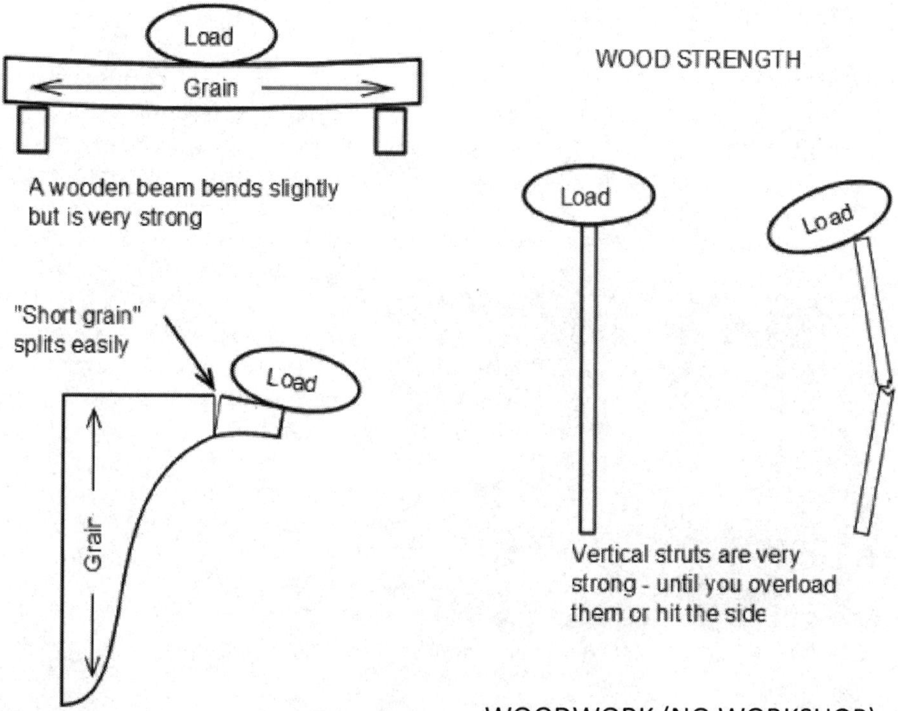

use it outside and it gets wet it will warp the other way, and back again as the weather changes. Quite a lot of traditional design is concerned with minimising warping, or the effects of it.

Cut a narrow strip along a piece of wood and it will be bendy but quite strong but if you cut a strip across a board it won't take much to snap it along the grain.

Glue has been used for thousands of years, but if you put glue on the end of a piece of wood, all those empty hollow fibres do what they have evolved to do and drink it up. Sticking wood end-on with glue is generally not a great idea, though modern, thick, gap-filling glues are better than the old liquid types.

There's another snag with glue though. It only sticks to the surface. One well known brand used to advertise that it was 'stronger than the wood itself' which sounds quite impressive, but isn't. If you break a glued joint the fibres on the surface of the wood just separate from those next to them. Traditional joints in woodwork were all designed to bring the pieces of wood together so substantial areas of each piece were in contact, taking the load. Glue was only there to hold them in position with the shape of the wood making the joint strong.

DIFFERENT PRINCIPLES

Wood hasn't changed much since humans have been using it, apart from the fact that we are now forced to use rubbish quality because the good stuff doesn't grow fast enough for our needs. The big change in the last few decades has been in adhesives. They are now stronger, better at filling gaps and more waterproof than ever. This makes it feasible to laminate together layers of thin cheap wood to make shapes that previously would have been cut from a solid piece. More glue, less joinery.

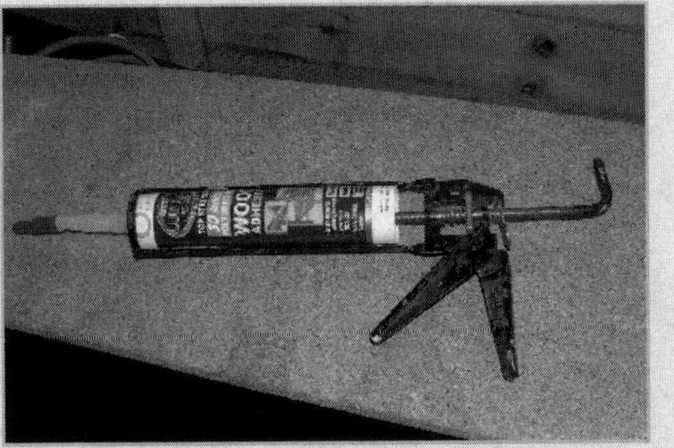

Polyurethane glue is ideal for rough woodwork.

The jobs featured here use either weatherproof PVA, or polyurethane. The latter is stronger, 100% waterproof and dries more quickly, but it's more expensive. It comes in cartridges as a gel, but foams slightly and expands into gaps.

Some principles remain.

Sticking end grain isn't a good idea, unless it's dead flat, a large area and you aren't going to put much strain on it. And wood still splits and warps.

TASKS FOR THE RUFFIAN WOODWORKER

Workbench Restoration

My Workmate is very, very old. It's had a hard life too, being left out in the rain too often, used as a platform for building and decorating tasks and as a saw-horse for chain-sawing logs. If you pick up a cheap one in a sale it could well look much the same, so the first task is to make a new top for it.

The top surfaces of a Workmate double as vice jaws, so they need to resist compression. Wood isn't great at that, at least not on the side as all those empty fibres just tend to squash. It's much better if you turn it around and use the end grain, after all that was strong enough to support a tonne or more of tree.

However, a narrow board cut across the grain will split, so the answer is to laminate two layers together, one running sideways across the width of the top to resist splitting, and a top layer made of short pieces laid at right angles so the end grain forms the vice jaws. To make it even better, two layers of typical pallet wood is just about the ideal thickness (but pallets do vary, so you might have to search around a bit).

Start by finding suitable wood for the bottom layer. On this design one piece of pallet was just right for the moving jaw, and two for the fixed (back) one. Make them a bit too long so you can trim them later.

Glue the back two together to make the right width (or a bit over). If the workbench still works with the old tops you can use it to clamp these together. If you don't have the original 'stops' to hold wide work, just nail a strip of wood to each top and use those to squeeze the board together. Take care to keep the boards flat though when you clamp them. If necessary screw them down to the old bench top 'til the glue dries. I used 'Lumberjack' polyurethane on this because it's quick and strong.

If the old bench top is beyond use you have a couple of options. If you have a piece of chipboard, ply or MDF bigger than the top you are making, assemble it on that. Lay paper on it so the work doesn't stick and nail or screw two strips of

WORKBENCH TOP

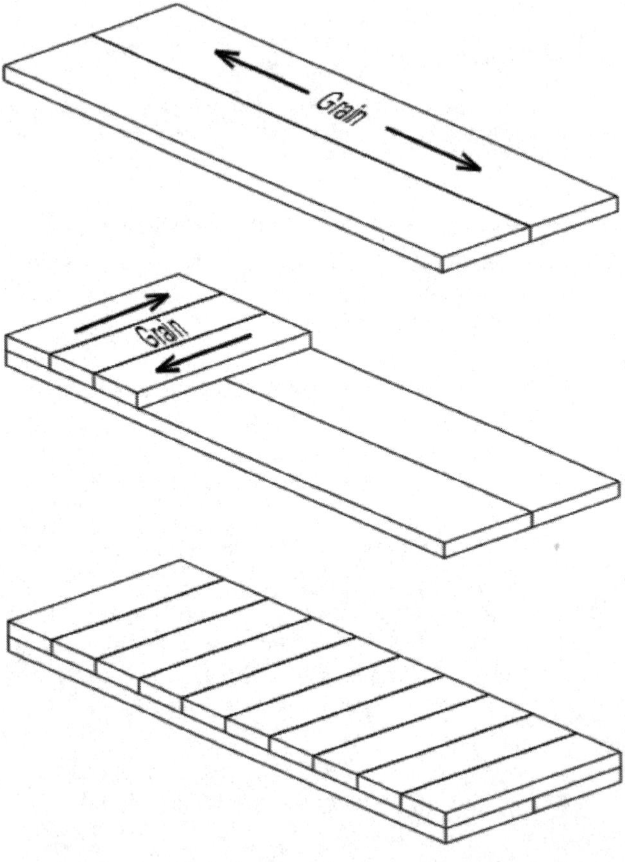

Glue two boards to make up correct width

When dried add cross boards one at a time

Trim edges and fit to workbench

wood either side of those you are joining, leaving gaps around 10mm wide. Now make some wedges and drive them between these strips and the work.

If you don't have a suitable board, use a pallet, or even strips taken from a pallet. The principle's the same.

While that's drying, cut all the short top pieces. Choose decent bits of pallet for this, avoiding knots, splits and nail holes. Cut them all slightly longer than the width of the top you're making.

Glue one piece at a time.

Glue one piece at a time and clamp it. If you have lots of clamps carry on and do the rest, making sure they are as close as possible to their neighbours. I don't have many clamps so I did one at a time and left it to dry while I did something else.

When all the glueing is done and well dried, trim the new tops to the same size as the old ones. A plane is handy, but not essential if you can saw straight.

Restored workbench in use.

The fittings vary on different makes and models, but it's not rocket science. Unscrew the old tops and copy any holes/slots needed, but before you screw on the new ones, give them a good seeing to with wood preserver. Mine are done in true ruffian style with Creocote, but you'd get a better finish with clear Cuprinol followed by varnish. Creocote tends to 'bleed' into any new wood it comes into contact with.

Compost Bin (1)

Three pallets, a couple of boards and some nails...

A front made from the fourth pallet.

Detail of pegged corner joint.

I'm keen on pallet wood for garden projects. It's free (always a plus point), mostly pretty strong, though some has large knots and weird grain that make it prone to snapping in odd places, and the roughness of it looks right in a garden, especially once it's discoloured a little. This project uses pallets with the minimum amount of modification.

You will need a minimum of five pallets, and an extra one would be handy. They don't all need to be the same, but you need at least two pairs.

The back panel is a pallet 'au nature'. The sides are pallets with the lower boards removed so they will hook around the back one as shown. Some pallets are like this anyway, so there might be even less work.

The front takes a bit of effort though. I made a compost bin in a hurry years ago by lashing together four pallets. The compost was fine, but a beggar to get out. It's much easier if you can remove the front.

Set up the first three pallets and fix the back corners with big nails. Now dismantle a spare pallet to get some boards long enough to go across the front. Nail a couple on, one at ground level and the next one on top of it. Add more if you wish. It will make it stronger, but harder to shovel compost out.

Take your fourth pallet and remove all the skids so you just have the deck. It sounds easy but in practice you might wreck it, which is where the spare one comes in handy to replace the snapped bits! You might also need to adjust the size a bit so it will drop down between the sides and behind the front planks.

At this point it looks usable, but if you started shovelling weeds in they'd soon force the sides outwards. What it needs is pegs to hold the sides to the front. Strong, steel pegs made from 125-150mm (5" or 6") nails.

First find your nails, then a suitable drill just a little bit bigger. Drill though the front panel and into the corner block at each side, near the top. Don't drill too deep though. Remove the front and fit a smaller drill, then drill the corner blocks deeper. If you don't pilot drill for nails this size you run the risk of splitting the blocks.

Bang the nails in, leaving them sticking out about 30-40mm. A good tip when banging nails into anything a bit flimsy and likely to move is to hold something heavy against the opposite side of the work piece to absorb some of the force. An engineering brick, a lump of rock or a sledge hammer all work well.

Saw the heads off and file the edges smooth. Drop the front in and pull it forwards to sit on the pegs. Now you can use it.

To remove the front just bang it backwards off the pegs and lift it.

Compost Bin (2)

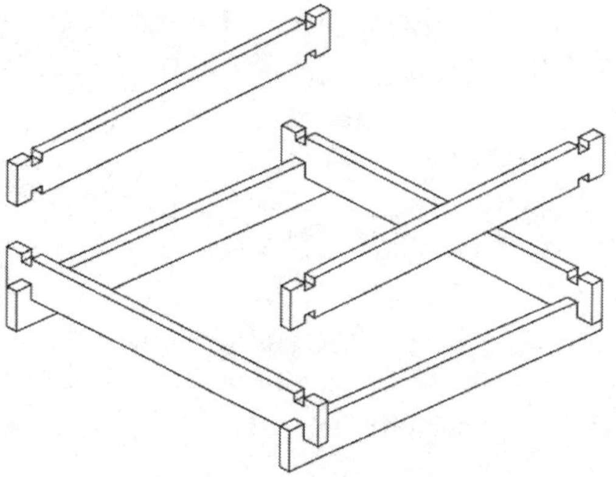

You can adapt the design to suit any available boards.

I cribbed this one from the bins on sale in many garden centres and DIY stores. You can make it any size you want, but the basic idea is to cut notches in the boards so they slot together. If you cut a quarter of the width in from each side, the boards will all touch. Cut a bit less and you get gaps.

To make the slots, cut down both sides with a saw, then place a chisel across the bottom and give it a whack.

Obviously you have to be moderately careful to make sure all the joints line up. If you have a stash of boards in different lengths it might work out better to make a rectangular bin rather than a square one. Just remember to make an equal number of long and short boards.

You will need a pair of half width boards for the bottom, and an optional pair for the top if you want it neat. Unlike the rough pallet job above, it's easy to fit a nice hinged lid to this design, just make sure you fit it to the last complete board, not the half width strip on the top that will come off too easily.

Even old floor boards will last ten years outside.

I made this ruinous looking bin from old floorboards ten years before the photo was taken. If you use pressure-treated boards it should last twice that. Decking boards would be good. I slapped some fence paint on the boards when I first made it, but after a year or two it had mostly gone. Re-coating it might have preserved it a little longer.

You don't actually empty bins made this way, you just dismantle them from around the compost and rebuild them alongside ready to start again.

You could make a small, neat compost bin from pallet wood using this technique, but it would be too small for our wilderness.

Soil Sieve

Our soil is full of stones, and compost made from our weeds is usually full of stones too, and half digested roots. For rough gardening it's usable, but if you want something finer for seeds or cuttings you need a soil sieve.

Once again there are no exact measurements for this. It depends on your strength, the availability of cheap/free wood and the size of any mesh you have available. Again pallet wood is fine, or anything about 70-100 (3-4") wide and around 20mm (¾") thick.

Nails and screws don't work very well into end grain as they tend to slide between the wood fibres, encouraging it to split. Even if the wood doesn't split they don't grip well and the joint will probably come apart, especially in something like this where you are going to be shaking it a lot. The answer is corner blocks; pieces of wood as long as the sides are wide, and about 40mm (1½") square.

Sieving out the stones to give the plants a chance.

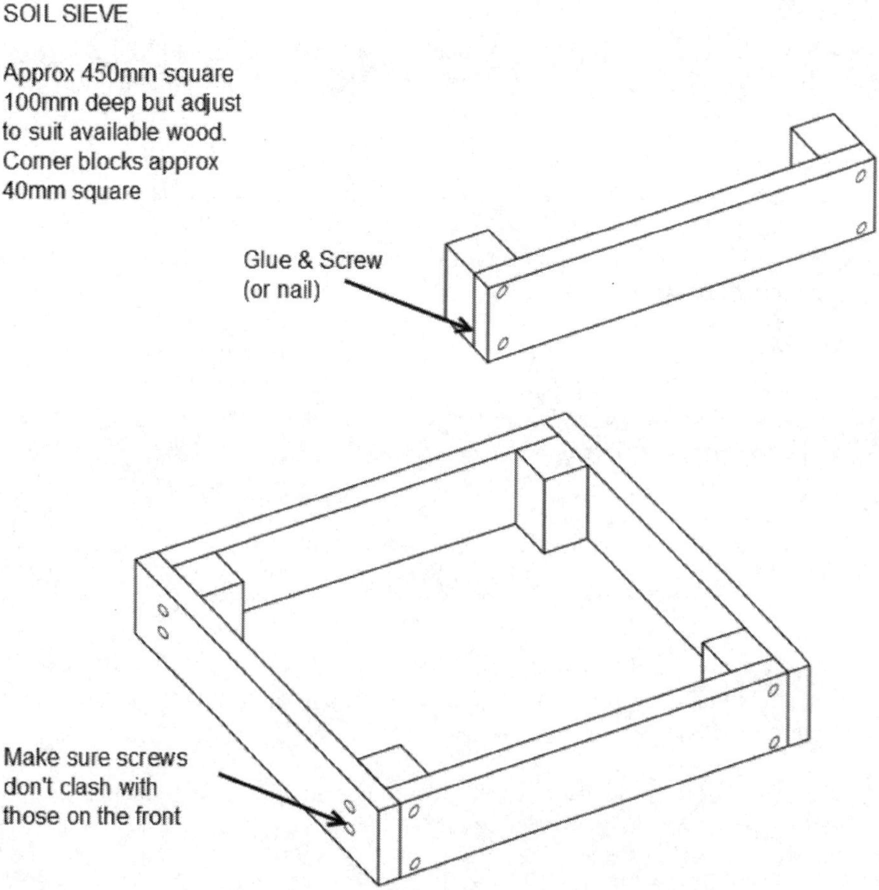

Fix the blocks with screws, or screws and glue if you want it to be really strong. Make sure the screws from the side don't clash with those from the end. Corner blocks like this are the answer to a lot of rough woodwork. Boxes, shelving, steps and frameworks can all be strengthened using blocks.

The sieve mesh is sold for pet cages with different hole sizes for different pets. The one in the photo is 1" x ½" which is OK for use on the garden, but too coarse for potting. ½" square would be better for that. I fixed the mesh using a staple gun that takes heavy duty ∩ shaped staples. If you don't have one you can buy staples to hammer in, or even use small nails and bend them over the mesh.

Fold the mesh a little way up the sides of the frame and staple it there. It's much stronger that fixing it to the bottom of the frame where the weight of soil (and stones) will tend to pull the staples out. Snip the mesh at the corners so you can fold it round neatly.

Shed Building

When I was at college the allegedly academic students training to teach English, geography and so on coined the term 'Shedbuilders' for us Design & Tech students. At the last count we had six sheds here, two for tools, one for my office and three for wood, though two are really just lean-to shelters to keep the rain off our logs. Maybe the academics were right.

Once again I'm not giving hard and fast designs. Sheds, like any great architecture, should fit the site and reflect the owner's taste and lifestyle, which in my case is scruffy and cheap. A simple log store is a good place to start, especially if you have a convenient wall to build it against.

Lean-to Log Store

This is just a roof with one edge attached to an existing wall and a couple of legs to support the other side. Scale it up a bit and you have an outside work area, a car port or, if you live in sunnier climes, a verandah.

Fixing the roof to the wall is the only technical bit and if you don't do it properly it will come away. There are two methods:

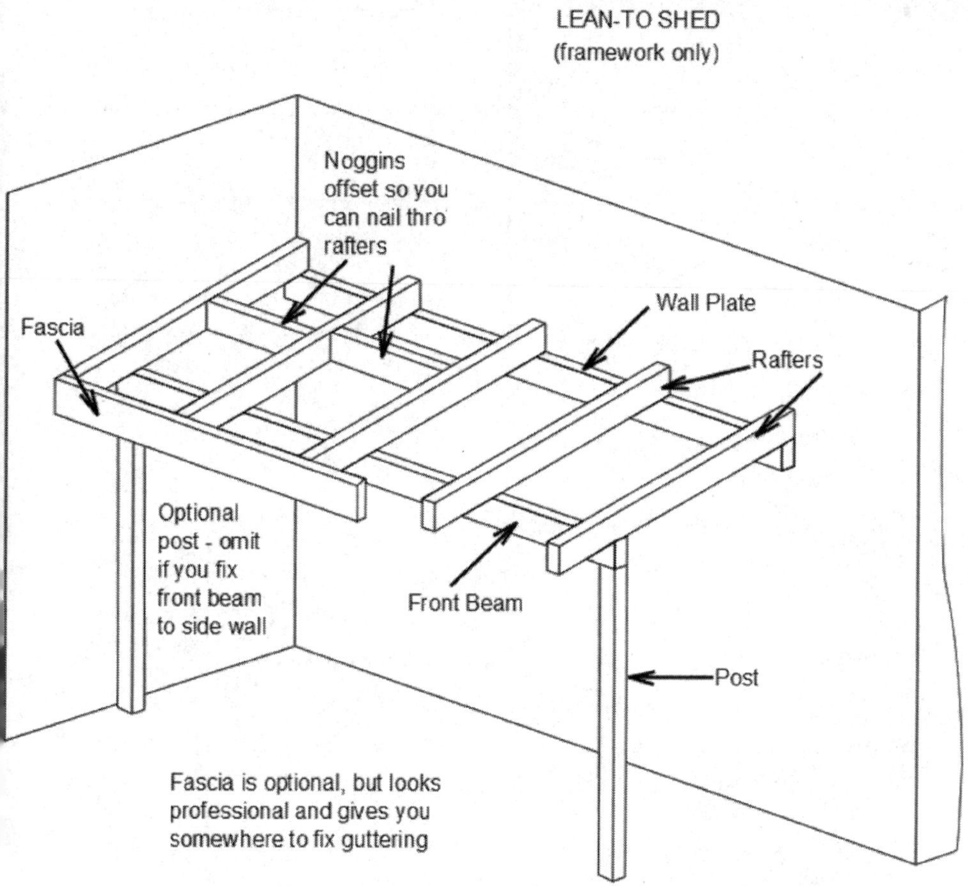

1. *Attach a piece of timber as a wall plate and fix the roof joists to that*
2. *Attach each joist direct to the wall, probably with some ironwork*

Wallplates

Wallplates are common for sheds, but must be done well. The drawings overleaf shows what can happen if they aren't.

If you have a good, strong brick or block wall then you can use frame fixings - big

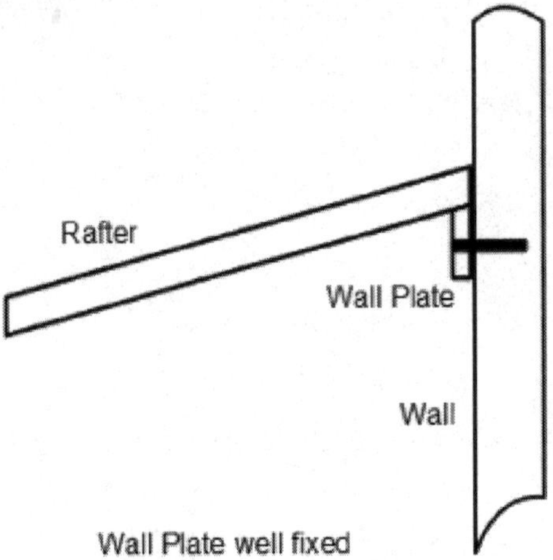

screws that come fitted into really big plastic wall plugs. For a basic log store 3 x 2" is suitable for the wall plate and you'll need 150mm fixings and a very long drill.

Unlike normal 'Rawlplugs' where you drill a hole, bang the plug in, then hold the wood in place while you insert the screw, frame fixings come with the screw already fitted part way into the plastic plug.

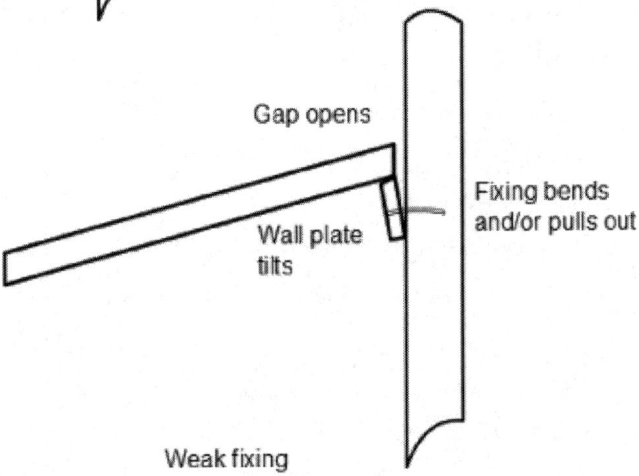

You need a drill big enough to allow the plug body to slide through, but not the screw head or the countersunk bit at the end of the plastic. And it should be a drill that can go through both wood and masonry. The technique is simple. Hold the wood in place, drill through it into the wall, push the fixing in and tighten the screw. Cowboys use a 'Birmingham Screwdriver' (a hammer) to whack the screw in. It is faster but not as strong.

If you don't have a masonry drill long enough, use a wood drill first, then mark the wall through the hole. Remove the wood and drill the wall with a masonry drill.

Frame fixings don't work well in rubble walls. What looks like a decent stone might turn out to be only 3cm deep and soft or brittle. The mortar will definitely be soft and crumbly. So it's back to the old way.

Mark where the wood is going to go. Chalk works well on old walls, but you can often find a bit of brick or slate or similar that will mark stone.

You are going to use small pieces of wood fitted into the mortar lines as plugs that you can nail or screw into, so seek out some likely looking lines near each end and at roughly 60cm intervals. Chisel out the mortar to about 10cm deep, or more if the wall is very soft. Cut a piece of softwood slightly larger than the hole and bang it in. If the wall is in bad condition you might need to point around the plug with cement.

Fix the wall plate with nails or screws – as long as possible, the further they go into the wall the better. Fix the joists to the wall plate with long nails – but pre-drill first as whacking 6" nails into the wallplate can loosen it.

JOIST HANGERS AND OTHER METALWORK

As the name suggests, these are often used to hang floor joists. They can be screwed to an existing wall or built into a new wall as it goes up. Basically they are a long strip of galvanised steel folded so that they provide a horizontal shelf on which your joist rests, and two long strips that can be fixed to a wall with rawlplugs, or bent to hang on a course of bricks/blocks before the next course is added.

Joist hangers are a bit over the top for most sheds, but useful if you are building a 'lean-to' extension. They don't provide any lateral support to tie your roof to the wall, so unless something else anchors it, avoid them.

If it's a small, light shed then you could use steel shelf brackets to support the joists, or if you have access to some strip steel, a hammer and a drill, make your own.

Front Beam

For a simple rectangular shed you need a front beam the same size as the wall plate with a leg near each end. If the shed is more than a couple of meters long though, 3",x,2" will sag unless there is something supporting it. You have a choice; a third leg or a deeper beam. It doesn't have to be thicker, just deeper. If you're not sure, prop the beam up on a couple of bricks and stand on it. If it sags more that a few millimetres, get a wider one.

Legs

The front of the shed is propped up with a couple of legs (more if it's very long). Since the weight of the roof bears straight down they don't need to be especially strong, but they will look ridiculous if they are too thin, and sooner or later you'll stumble against one or hit it with a wheelbarrow and bring the whole roof down. 3" x 3" is a popular choice.

What you do about the bottom of the legs depends on the terrain. If the wood is 'tanalized' and you are building on soil, you could just dig a hole, put a flattish rock at the bottom to spread the load and stop the wood sinking, build on that and then shovel the soil back in. It should last 20 years.

If you are building on a concrete yard, digging a hole isn't easy. Fortunately, it's not necessary either. The simplest solution is to rest the post on the concrete and fix it with a steel bracket or two. You could even make a wooden bracket from a natural cruck. See the next chapter for more about that. Or you can get cunning.

One cunning answer is to drill a hole in the concrete and grout in a short length of steel (reinforcing bar – re-bar - is ideal) Then drill a hole in the end of the post to fit onto it. Another one I've used is to recycle an adjustable foot from some old office racking. You can probably invent alternatives based on what junk you have. You just need something to secure the post so a collision with a wheelbarrow doesn't bring the roof down.

Roofing Material

There's no end of different materials you can use. For most of us cost and convenience outweigh other considerations and that is normally wood and felt. For large areas ½" shuttering ply is usually the cheapest, and being designed for use with concrete it's also water resistant. If you have some old floorboards or tongue & groove cladding available, use it. Providing you cover it in roofing felt before it gets wet, it will last for ages.

Roofs need to slope and even 'flat' roofs slope a bit to make sure the rainwater and snow melt runs off. 2-3cm per metre is about the least you can get away with, but if you are buying new roofing material, check the manufacturer's recommendations.

Supporting the Roof

Corrugated steel sheet can span about a metre to 1.5M without intermediate supports but ½" ply cannot and will sag. As with the beams, if you aren't sure test it on ground level by standing on it.

There are conventions for joist/rafter spacing, but you can make up your own rules for rough sheds. With ply still made for the UK market in 4' widths, rafters on 2' centres work well – one under each joint and one in the middle of the sheet. If the board sags too much, use three per board on 16" centres.

With ½" ply you will need cross supports between the rafters too. The normal way of doing these is to make 'noggins' out of offcuts from the joists. Cut them to fit and nail them in.

Rather than try to line them up and have trouble banging nails in at an angle, just offset the noggins. However, if you are building a real mega-shed where the roof is wider than a single sheet of ply, then you will need a cross member under the joint. You can still use noggins, but you will need long nails knocked in diagonally from each side. This will be easier if you drill first.

If your lean-to shed is going in a corner between two walls, don't assume they are 'square' (at right angles). On old buildings they rarely are and if you cut all the wood 'correctly' you may well find it doesn't fit together properly. I find it a lot easier to lay out the roof frame on the ground in the corner where it is going to fit.

The joints between the posts and the rafters are vital. Nails are good for holding things in place, but not so great for supporting a load. They bend and come loose. Ideally you need the post under the rafters to support the weight, rather than be simply nailed to the side of them.

The problem is that when you have a corner post you usually have a rafter and a front beam coming together, and both need to rest on the post. The top of the post may not be big enough. If it isn't then a block screwed (not nailed) to the side of the post gives a bit more room. It's also a useful dodge if the front beam and rafters are not the same depth. You can position the block higher or lower, as required.

Supporting blocks don't have to look like a bodge and with a bit of effort they can actually become a feature!

Roofing Felt

Shuttering ply might be water resistant, in the sense that the plies are stuck with water-proof adhesive, but it will rot, and the joints will leak. You need to cover it. Roofing felt is traditional for sheds, but you can get neoprene too.

Felt comes in various grades, depending on use. The lightest (and thus cheapest) is sometimes called underlay because in proper built-up roofing it is used under a heavier layer (called a capsheet) which is finished with a fine layer of gravel (manufacturers call it 'mineral'). A single layer of the light stuff is suitable for a small shed and a single layer of capsheet will do for bigger sheds. I've never felt the need to get into two or three layer built-up roofing.

Nails, Adhesive or both?

You can fix felt with special nails called clouts that have very large heads and are very short so they don't go right through the roof boards. Clouts work well enough on sloping roofs but when a roof is nearly flat water has a tendency to seep under the seams, so it's a good idea to use a bitumen based roofing-felt adhesive on the seams. Even on sloping roofs sticking the seams down extends the life of the felt by preventing the wind worrying away at the edges until it rips or the clouts pull through. This is especially true of the ridge on conventional sheds.

With any kind of roofing, start at the bottom and work up so the overlaps face the right way.

A problem area on lean-to roofs is where they join the wall on which they lean. At the very least, you need to turn the felt up a few inches and glue it to the wall. If the shed abuts a brick wall you can make a much better joint by raking out a mortar line just above the shed roof level and tucking the felt into it. Then seal it with bituminous mastic, a black gunk you can get in tins or cartridges for mastic guns. You can do this on a stone wall too, but with random stone you will need a large angle grinder to cut the groove.

Shingles are smarter than felt.

Shingles come in metre-log strips.

Nail just above the split between shingles.

Felt Shingles

Real slate or tiles are a bit over the top for the average shed, and heavy too, so you need to build a much stronger roof to support them. But if you want a smarter roof without too much expense or trouble, shingles are good.

They come in metre-long strips, each made up of four shingles, but you can cut them easily if necessary. They are stronger than normal felt, with a glass fibre layer to stop them tearing. All the usual DIY stockists have them.

Start with a set of shingles reversed, or some edging strip available from the same stockists, then a row of shingles. Nail them down with clouts positioned just above the notch, then make the next layer cover the nails. The shingles each have a strip of adhesive already applied and covered with a removable plastic layer. The adhesive doesn't seem very sticky, but it's a kind of tar that softens and sticks when the sun shines. For awkward areas you can use normal felt adhesive.

If you have a ridge on your shed you can use the edging strip again, or as above, cut the sheets into single shingles and lap them.

If you've built a lean-to shelter, nailing some kind of boarding to the posts turns it into a proper shed. Shuttering ply works well here too, but it is pretty ugly, which is OK if the shed is out of sight like my number two tool shed. This one is round the back where I saw logs and split them for the fire. It's hidden from the house and the best bits of the garden and is just somewhere secure to keep a chain saw, splitting maul, axe and a few other heavy duty tools (concrete mixer, pick, sledgehammer, shovel – just normal gardening tools round here!)

It's an odd shape but useful to demonstrate some techniques. On one side is a brick wall separating this working area from the 'nice' part of the garden .At the back is a concrete retaining wall (See soil page 6) which is 1.4M high and not quite square to the brick wall. At the other side the concrete wall turns 45°, giving the shed a sort of wedge shape. I acquired some doors from Freecycle, leaving about 90cm to plank to complete the front, and I needed to add something on top of the concrete wall to make it a bit higher.

As you can see in the photos, there's a wall plate fixed to the brick wall on the right. There are stubby posts fixed to the concrete wall with frame fixings to support the back and left-hand side. There's a beam across the front that's 100mm deep since it has to span a double door arrangement, and posts on which to hang the doors. To save work and cash the front beam doubles as a fascia, the joists are nailed to it rather than resting on it. You can do this with small, light shed roofs. The same applies at the back and side too.

It's a sort of shed...

The right-hand post is fixed to the brick wall, but the other is a little trickier. Doors put quite a load on posts as when you open the door it tends to push the bottom of the post backwards unless it is well fixed. This shed is built on a concrete yard area, so the post is fixed to a horizontal plate that is screwed down into the concrete. To help keep the framework dry I laid a row of bricks under the beam too.

Drill the plate and post.

If you fix the beam to the floor first you then have the problem of how to nail the post to it. So a better method is shown here. Fix the post, or in this case two posts, to the plate first.

The back and left walls are just ply like the roof, and I even covered them in roofing felt and glued it down to the top of the concrete.

The short bit of wall at the front is a bit more interesting though. It's made of pallets. If you just nail boards horizontally water will penetrate the joints and encourage the wood to rot, so you need to make the edge of each plank slope down at the front. For a small project like this you can plane them by hand, putting an angle of about 15° on both sides of each plank. No, I didn't measure it, and as long as they all look about the same they'll be fine. It's a tool shed.

Nail the post to the plate before you fix it to the floor.

I coated each board with Creocote before nailing it on to make sure there was a good coating inside the joints. As with roofing, start from the bottom, but don't put the bottom plank on the floor. Overlap the beam at the bottom of the frame slightly so that water running down the wall runs onto the brick foundation.

You could use the same technique on much bigger sheds, but I wouldn't fancy planing that many boards. A circular saw with the blade canted over would be much quicker. It's only a small step then to 'shiplap' boarding.

Shed Floors

Crude lean-tos usually manage with whatever floor they find themselves standing on. One step up from that is, you guessed it, pallets. If you store logs on the ground, the bottom layer or two will never dry out, certainly not in the UK. Make a base of pallets and you get drier logs. Incidentally, stacking logs against a house wall can lead to damp problems in the house, so it's quite a good idea to put some pallets upright against the house to create an air space too.

Better sheds need better floors, and once again shuttering ply is hard to beat, laid on 3 x 2" tanalized joists for a quality job, or on pallets for a quick and cheap one. Large sheds are usually built on a solid foundation of some sort (See chapter four - hard surfaces), and the floor laid inside the complete shed.

Smaller, lighter sheds can be built like the flat pack ones from a DIY store where a wooden floor is laid on bricks or slabs and the walls placed on top of the floor, and fixed down onto it. With such a light construction this usefully adds the weight of the contents to that of the construction, making it less likely to blow away in a gale!

Free-standing Sheds

Lean-tos are quick and easy but real sheds can stand up by themselves. There are hundreds of variations, but basically only two methods.

1. You make a framework and clad it
2. You make walls flat on the floor, raise them up and fix them together.

In rough and ready building it depends on what materials you have. Frameworks need to be strong enough to stand up and tolerate you banging hundreds of nails into them when you plank it. If you plank your walls on the floor they can be much lighter. The whole thing gains strength once all the walls, floor and roof are fixed together. This is the method the DIY stores use to make flat-pack sheds.

Framing is in some ways easier. You can develop the design as you build, and it's not really much different to building a lean-to. 'Scant' 3 x 2" softwood and 5" nails are suitable for most frames.

Raised sheds need to be designed properly and built accurately or they won't fit together. The key thing to get right is how the corners fit together (See Drawing). If you are planning something like this, go and have look at some ready made ones in a store. A few minutes checking out how other people do it can save a lot of puzzlement later.

PRE-FAB SHED WALL DETAILS

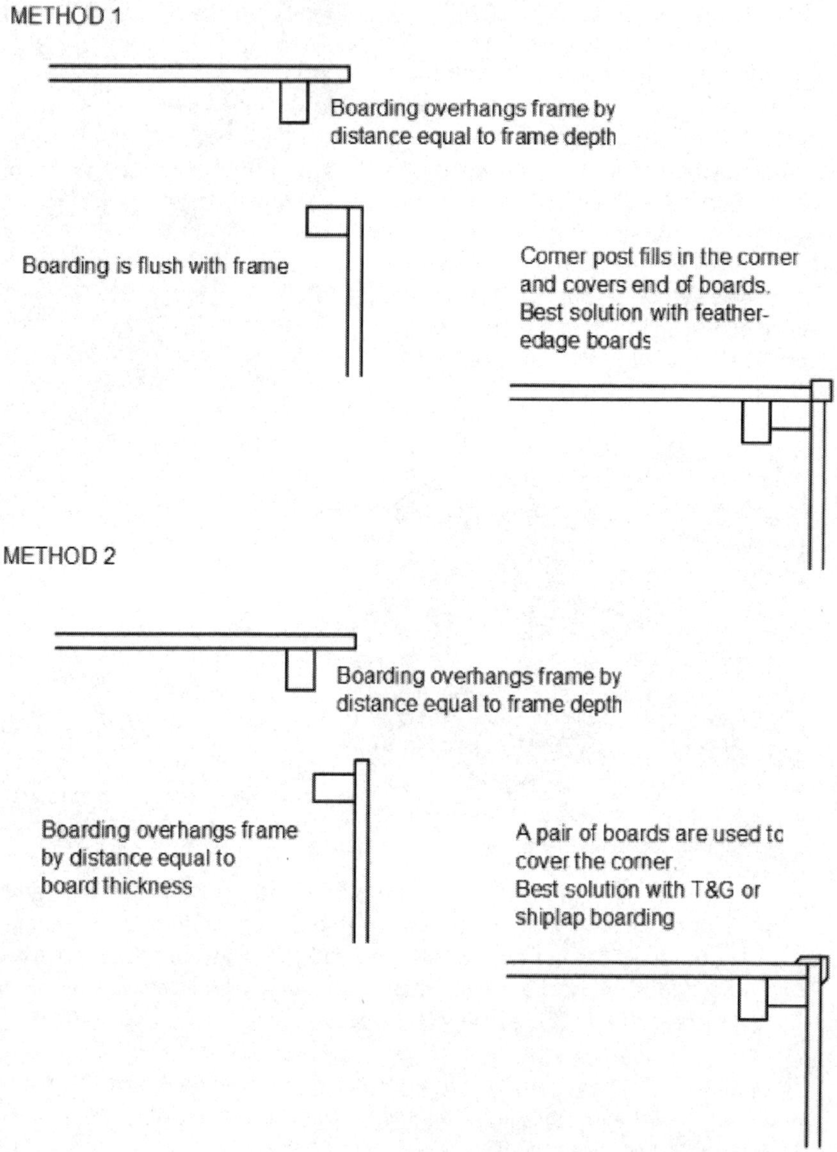

The US 'barn raising' technique is interesting. Basically you build four walls flat on the floor, then get all your mates round (beer is usually provided as an inducement) to hoist them up and hold them while you fix the corners together. The snag is that most of us don't have a prairie to work on and there's no room for four walls to be laid out flat in most gardens.

An alternative is to make the floor first, then build one wall on the floor, hoist it up and prop it somehow. Build the second wall, raise it and fix it to the first. The third and fourth walls are a challenge since if you fix the third, the space is now too small to work in, so you need to prop it out of the way. When building my office I thought all this through, considered the Welsh weather and the likelihood of a gale wrecking part-built walls and decided to get a specialist shed builder to pre-fab the walls in his workshop!

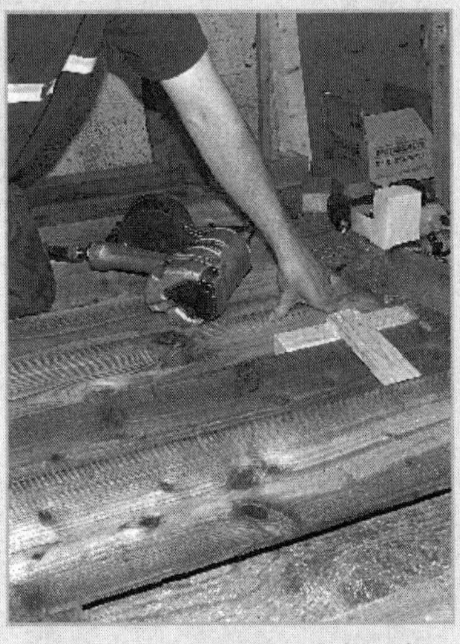

A cunning gadget to set board spacing – and a nail gun.

Assembling pre-fab shed walls. Side wall is low so the rafters can rest on it.

Boarding

Modern mass produced sheds are usually made with 'shiplap' boarding, that is boards that have been milled with a rebate on one edge (the lower one when you nail it on) and a moulding on the other edge that makes it thin enough to fit into the rebate of the next board. It has several advantages; you can use very thin boards, each board lies flat, making the corners easy to manage, the inside is smooth and neat and the outside is attractively textured.

For a similar price you can also buy tongue & groove (T&G) boards that slot together, the tongues pointing up to shed any rainwater.

Feather-edge board has a tapered cross-section.

Both shiplap and T&G are the product of industrial wood milling In an earlier age boards were just rip sawn from a log. To make them easier to lap they were, and still are, often cut with a slight taper. On a 150mm board the thickness will vary from around 25mm down to 6mm. You nail them on thin edge up and lapped by about 10-20mm.

You see boards like this on old barns and they certainly look better than shiplap on large sheds in rural settings. Most are painted black simply because from around the mid-nineteenth century farmers used to get cheap tar from the gasworks and slap it on everything. Prior to that they were either natural or painted with whatever was to hand, so unless your council or conservation area insist on black, paint it any colour you want.

The big drawback with such 'feather-edge' boards is that only the first (bottom) board lies flat on the frame. All the others are canted a bit, leaving gaps that look messy inside and make it essential you do something clever in the corners to avoid the wind blowing in. The usual answer is a substantial piece of wood fitted into the corner.

Windows

Old-style allotment sheds seem mostly to have evolved around whatever windows and doors were available. There's nothing wrong with that if you can find some in good condition. The windows in my office (which is just a big shed) are double glazed units from a house that was being extended. Unfortunately you might not be able to find the right size windows at the right time, so it's useful to know how to make rough and ready window frames.

Once again, we're relying on the properites of modern adhesive to overcome deficiencies in timber and joinery techniques. This window was made from pallet wood using only very basic tools and a Workmate bench.

As with the bench top (see page 67), the key thing is to laminate the two layers together, in this case to enable you to make lap joints, halving joints and rebates without any clever joinery. I hope the drawing makes it clear.

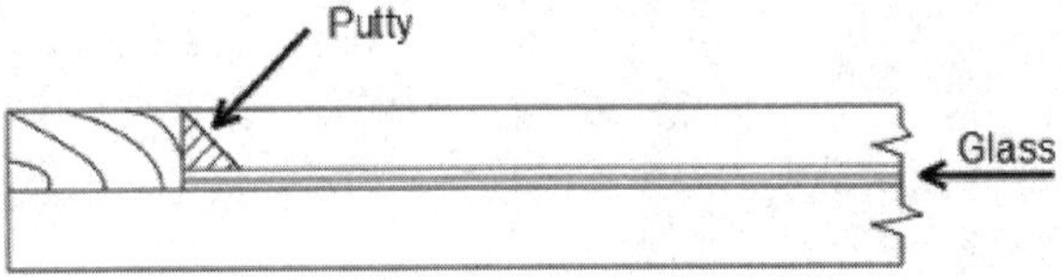

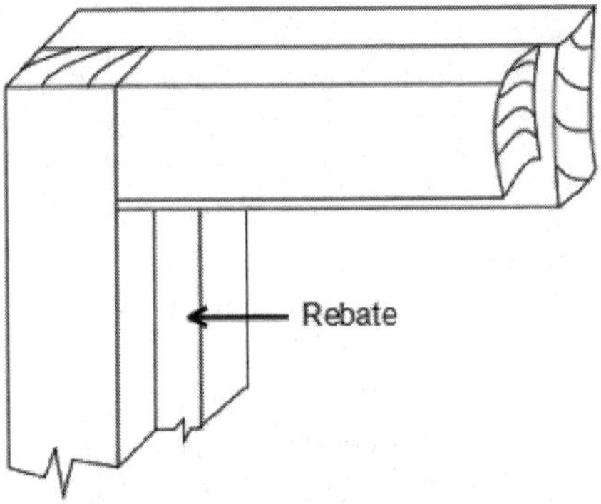

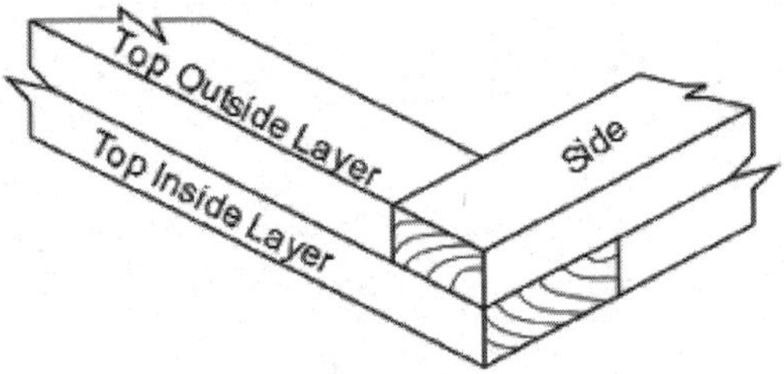

Basically the inside layer of wood is wider so when the outer piece is applied you get a rebate for the glass.

Side piece with inner layer wide and short, outer narrow and longer.

The other feature is that, whereas the side pieces on the inside layer are short with the top and bottom pieces fitted above and below, on the outside the side pieces are full height and the top and bottom fit between them. This creates halving joints at the corners.

That's all you need to know for a single pane window. To split it into a multi-pane design just use pieces of narrow and wide wood with the wide

Top piece with inner layer wide and long to make lap joint.

one on the inside butted to the inner layer of the frame and the narrow one longer so it fits into the rebate.

An engineering brick makes a decent anvil for rough metalwork.

Top piece with outer layer narrow and short to make rebate.

Having made it, you will need to putty the glass in. Putty knives are all very well, but none works as well as a piece of 15mm copper pipe, flattened and curved as shown above.

Puttying with a a home-made putty tool.

Glued, nailed and checked with a try-square.

I made the window as a sample for the book. I don't need another shed at the moment, but it found another use combined with some old bricks as an impromptu cold frame. Maybe next year I'll scrounge some more pallets and make a proper job. Or maybe I'll need another shed by then, a workshop would be good...

Doors

Like windows, doors don't always turn up when you feel a shed coming on, so sometimes you have to make them.

The simplest is the ledge and brace design. The three horizontal bars are the ledges, the diagonals the braces. Fitted correctly the braces point upwards from the hinge side, supporting the ledges and preventing the door from sagging. You quite often see amateur doors mounted upside down and occasionally braces pointing both ways, one up and one down.

Glue and nail the boards to the first ledge.

Glue the brace and use temporary nails to hold it in place while you nail from the other side.

For a lightweight shed door you need T&G boards about 12mm (½") thick with ledges and braces about twice that thickness and about 70mm (3") wide. Unless you have a supply of free wood, it's easier and cheaper to buy a self assembly kit from a DIY store or builders' merchant. Wickes do a good one based on 3" boards that makes a maximum of 3'3" but can be reduced in 3" steps to 2'6". Sometimes, though, you need a heavy-duty door.

My office (See pages 60-61) has french windows which provide light in the summer, but also provide a tempting view of the contents and are impossible to secure, so just like the French I needed a shutter over them. It's cosier in the winter with the shutter shut too. To make a really secure job I built a heavy-duty ledge and brace door using 5 x 1" T&G and 6 x 1½" ledges and braces.

To make the ledges and braces appear a little less cumbersome I planed the edges to an angle, then to make sure the door didn't sag, I made joints between the ledges and braces. I've no idea if joints like this have a name, but I guess they are a form of housing. The shape is obvious from the photos, but not easy to figure out when both pieces of wood have sloping sides! All I can say to help is lay out the bits and draw what you have to cut out.

Tricky joints, but strong.

When laying out a big project like this you need a sheet of chipboard or similar to work on. Cover It with newspaper if you are gluing. I've read conflicting advice about glueing or not glueing T&G boards. In this case I didn't, but I glued and nailed the ledges and braces to the boards.

Assembly is a bit of a challenge since it is easier to lay it all out and glue it with the ledges up, but you need to nail through the T&G into the ledges and braces since they are thicker. I put it together upside down, tapped a couple of nails in each ledge and brace, then turned it over and finished it off from the right side.

Needless to say, the joints are not perfect. They are a bit gappy here and there, though they do touch where they need to in order to hold the door square. You can buy caulking for this, or you can stuff them with a mix of glue and sawdust or shavings.

Framed Doors

The shutters in the these photos were made for the house, not for a garden shed, but they do show a useful technique you can adopt for all sorts of doors and gates. Like the window they are laminated, though in this case from three layers of PAR (planed all-round, ie. smooth) softwood.

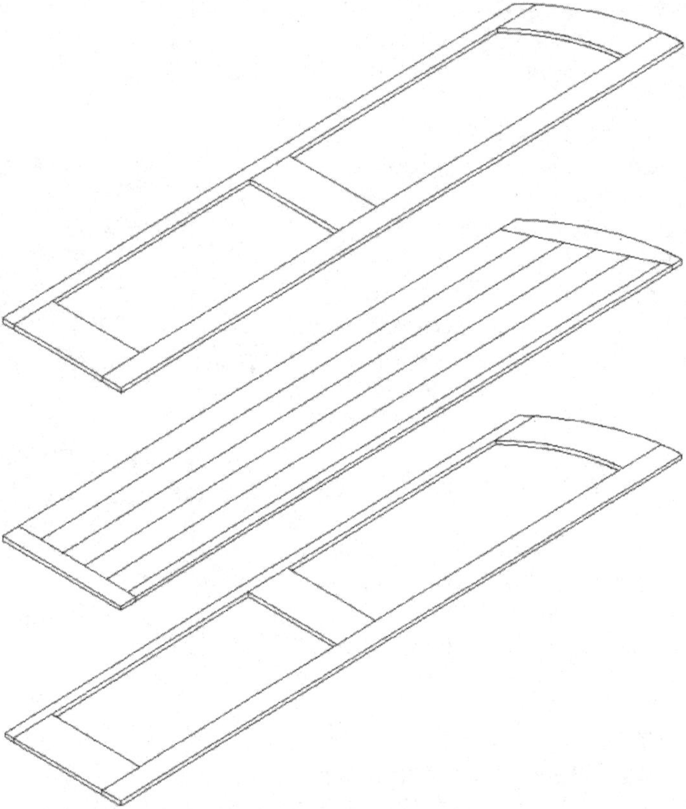

Shutter Layers

Left - First layer assembled and wedged in place on chipboard base.

Right - Three layers glued and nailed (with 1" panel pins).

As with the window design, the trick is to make the layers such that the joints overlap at the corners. Hopefully the photos and drawings make it clear. This time I glued the T&G. Assembly was carried out on a sheet of chipboard in several stages over a few days so each stage was dry before the next was added.

Posh Fence
(or Balustrade, if you prefer)

The ballustrade turns this from a danger zone to a chill-out spot.

I looked at a lot of fences before making this one for our terrace. Mass produced ones come in panels with fixed widths The length of our terrace was fixed by several immovable features and nothing would fit without substantial work. The only commercial alternative is the kind of balustrade you see round decking and I didn't fancy that.

Like many of my designs this uses layers of thin timber to create complex pieces and avoid traditional joint cutting, but I'm not pedantic about it. It also uses dowel joints and cross-halvings.

I'm not giving detailed drawings and cutting lists, but I hope by explaining the design process and the basic construction technique that you will be encouraged to design your own to suit your own situation.

I know this is billed as a rough and ready guide, but on this occasion you do need to do some planning. I drew my design on a computer, but you could use a pencil and paper. It must be accurate though.

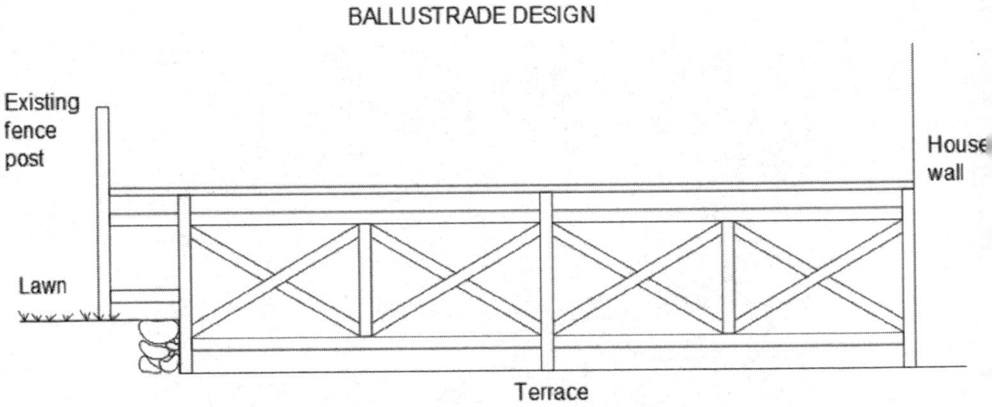

You will need an accurate drawing before tackling something like this.

The starting point is a scale drawing of the problem. In my case the fixed points are the house, the terrace itself which slopes slightly for drainage, and a small wall topped by a fence. Draw a line representing the position of the top rail. I wanted something sturdy to lean on while day dreaming, so it's a metre high. Waist height is comfortable for leaning on, less than hip height is too easy to fall over.

If you have young children around you will need to consider the size of the gaps in the design. Small children can almost squeeze their bodies through tiny gaps of as little as 100mm and then get their heads stuck. I wanted something with a more open appearance and as we don't have youngsters it's not really a problem. Any visitors will have to keep an eye on their offspring.

With the outline fixed, sketch in some alternatives. The advantage of using a drawing application on a computer is that you can generate dozens of different designs quickly. My balustrade is just over four metres long, so I soon came to the decision that I wanted one central post. Obviously this is one thing you will have to adjust to suit your own requirements. After playing around with horizontal rails, vertical palings and assorted diagonals, I decided on the crossed design shown, with a short vertical in the middle of each section.

Saw half-way through each just inside the lines and chisel out the joint.

Glue and clamp the crosses.

A DIY dowelling jig.

Like the shutters, this design uses PAR softwood laminated with waterproof PVA adhesive. The timber is nominally 4” x 1” but is actually 68 x 19mm. The main posts are made from three layers, the middle one designed to allow the rails to pass through, the crosses to slot in either side and a piece to protrude from the top to form a ‘tenon’ onto which the hand rail fits. The hand rail itself is made from 3” x 2”, which is actually 68 x 40mm.

The timber was delivered in 4.1 metre lengths, allowing the lower rail to be a single piece. The upper one is longer though, and joined in the middle, as is the hand rail.

The crosses are made with halving joints. To do this lay out the timbers and mark where they cross and cut as shown above.

To fix the crosses to the short upright I used dowel joints. You can get proper dowelling jigs for this but a piece of bent metal and a G clamp will do. Get an assistant to ‘sight’ the drill for you, telling you when it is perpendicular to the surface.

The post is secured at the house end with a 200mm screw into a large

200mm screw and giant plastic plug fixing.

plastic plug. The other end is attached to an existing fencepost. Both are fixed to the concrete terrace with steel brackets and rawlplugs. The middle post needs a strong bracket to hold it upright and I wanted to experiment with a 'grown knee' (See next chapter). A blacksmith-made steel bracket would look better.

WOOD FINISHING

Most woods soak up water[1], and once they are wet various wood-eating fungi move in and start devouring your work. The primary function of any wood finish outdoors is to keep the wood dry, and its second job is to poison fungi. Looking nice comes third.

PRESERVATIVES

Wood preservatives are oil based, very light and very 'watery', so they soak in well. As a consequence they are volatile and smell strongly. Fortunately outdoors the smell soon dissipates. Preservatives come in various colours and can be used by themselves to colour as well as preserve the wood. If you are going to varnish the wood afterwards, use a clear preservative. If you are going to paint it then use clear or a pale colour that won't show through the paint.

PAINT

For outdoor use there are two different types of paint, the traditional oil paints and the newer water based products marketed as shed paint or fence paint. For a quality job, like the balustrade above, then the ideal is preservative, primer, undercoat and gloss. You can save money by using a combined primer/undercoat. You will probably still need two coats but you'll only have half as many tins rusting away in the shed when you've finished.

You can use 'eggshell' or 'satin' instead of gloss if you want, but make sure it's a proper oil-based one. Acrylic (water based) paints are convenient indoors, but not so durable.

1 *Except naturally oily woods such as cedar and teak.*

Personally I detest thixotropic (non-drip) paints. They have a jelly-ish consistency in the tin, so a dollop of paint will stick to the brush and not drip. When you work it out on the wood it becomes liquid, in fact it rapidly becomes more liquid than liquid paint, making it prone to running on vertical surfaces.

Despite what the makers say about a paint's 'one coat' ability, it doesn't stick to the previous layer as well as a proper undercoat and it doesn't contain as much pigment, so it doesn't cover contrasting colour very well.

Shed/fence paint is for rough work, so don't expect a smooth, shiny finish from it. You will need a couple of coats on new wood, and it needs re-coating every few years to keep it looking fresh.

CHAPTER 9

WOODWORK (RUSTIC)

Modern woodwork normally uses seasoned (dried) timber that has been sawn into useful planks and boards. These rustic projects hark back to an earlier time before sawmills when people just cut down trees (or lopped branches) and used the wood just as it came.

COPPICING AND POLLARDING

If you cut a tree down to a stump, there's a very good chance it will regenerate. It won't grow into a conventional looking tree, though. It will put out side shoots that will turn upwards, then grow straight up, trying to outdo each other in their quest for sunlight. The result is a lot of thin, usually straight-ish stems that you can harvest in just a few years. Pollarding is much the same, though in this case the tree is cut higher, around the point where the first major branches start. It's often done to town trees to produce a lollipop shape and keep them a manageable size. The resulting growth is similar, but not so easy to harvest.

Coppiced willow has been used for millennia for baskets, for sheep hurdles and even for the wattle in wattle and daub building. Having neither willows nor sheep I've never tried it, but we do have sycamores that grow like weeds and they coppice very well. Even when you are hoping the thing will die, it just keeps on sprouting!

PLANT SUPPORTS

If you have a few coppiced trees, you'll never buy garden canes again.

Poles about 25mm (1") in diameter make good tripods for beans.

About twice that and you can make supports for raspberry canes. Saw

Precision not needed.

Natural poles and wire support for raspberries.

a rough point on the end with a bow (log) saw and whack them in. If the ground is hard or stony, make a starter hole with a metal bar, or a well aimed pick.

To stop them leaning in when you tension the wire, cut a couple of shorter poles and use them as props, tied to the uprights with garden wire. Then run three or four wires between the uprights to support the raspberries.

Natural poles make good supports for newly planted trees too. To avoid damaging the roots, put the pole a couple of feet away from the tree trunk, leaning at about 45° to meet the tree just under where the branches start. Tie it with something soft, proper tree ties if you want, or a bit of old bike tyre inner-tube.

Miniature fruit trees can be surprisingly heavy croppers, and if you are lax about pruning them you can end up with the branches being weighed down to the ground, or even snapped off. The supports shown on the next page are cut from coppiced sycamore just at the point where the main shoot branches out. Leaving a few inches of each branch gives you 'fingers' that you can use to fit under the tree branches.

Natural poles are perfect for young trees too.

Unsurprisingly we have a lot of brambles, and fortunately I love blackberry and apple tarts and bramble jelly. What's not so

Natural forks are useful for propping tree branches.

good though is the way they like to spread right across the garden. A few years ago I sort of tamed some by training them into a hedge arrangement. To give them something to cling to I whacked some sycamore stakes in a line, about one every metre, leaning over a bit so the bramble shoots can grow up them. To make sure they got the idea I split the top of each stake a little way and slotted a bramble into it. After a couple of years it turned into a bramble hedge that we could take a pair of shears to in order to keep it more or less in shape.

SEATING

A few strategically placed logs make decent stools, ideal for tired gardeners in need of somewhere to rest and ponder the meaning of dandelions. If you have some really big logs and a powerful chainsaw you can make rustic chairs .

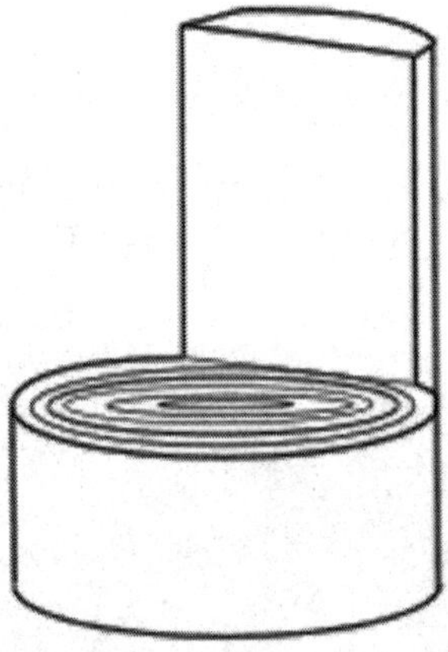

You need big logs and a big chainsaw to make chairs like this.

For us hill dwellers flat places where a log will stand up straight are limited, so a few years ago I built a log bench on a bank at the side of our lawn. It's a flower bed now and I haven't a decent photo, so here's a drawing.

I deliberately didn't fix the split log to the support. The plan was to remove the log every autumn and store it somewhere dry. I never did though.

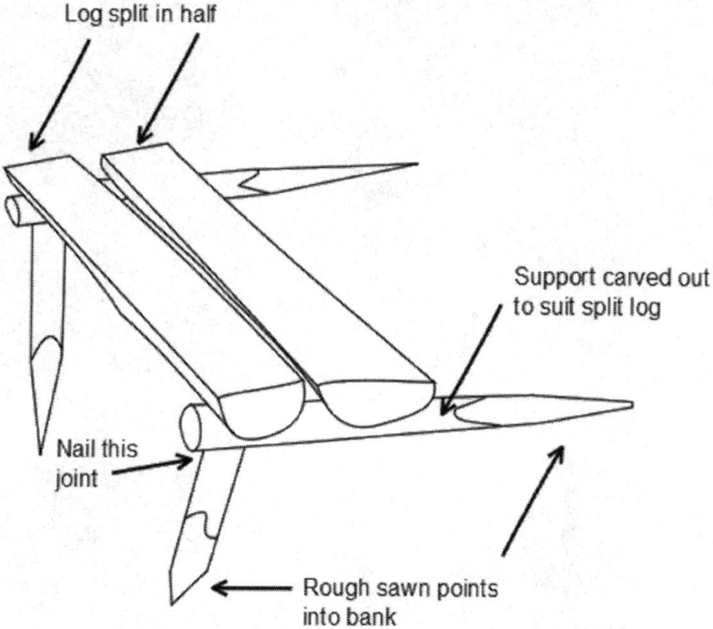

Splitting a log isn't easy. You need a steel wedge, a sledge hammer and a co-operative log with a straight grain. Mine didn't split at all easily, so I spent an hour trying to plane the split surface flat and smooth enough to sit on.

PATHS AND STEPS

We've already seen log steps (Page 46). If you are making a rustic path covered in bark or woodchippings then logs make an ideal natural edging. If your chainsaw is big enough, large rounds cut from a big log make attractive stepping 'stones' in a lawn. They aren't hugely practical though and are slippery when wet and rot quickly.

TIMBER FRAMING

Don't panic! I'm not going to launch into how to build a timber framed house, but sitting in a timber framed bar one evening I noticed how the corners of the frame were reinforced with brackets cut from a natural cruck. They are similar to what traditional wooden boat builders call 'grown knees'. In both cases they are used because the grain of the wood flows round the curve, giving it strength.

1

First find your knee. This isn't ideal but it will do.

2

Trim the log and work out the best place to cut.

3

With one cut made you can mark the second.

4

Then cut it.

5

If the log is wide enough you can trim the sides....

6

....like this.

It might be ugly, but it's strong.

Pondering over a pint or two, I thought it'd be fun to make one to support the balustrade post featured in the previous chapter. It turned out OK, but ugly. The second one is neater so when it's seasoned and preserved I might swap them.

These are made from sycamore, and it doesn't last well outdoors. To make them a bit more durable, take the roughly finished bracket indoors and leave it somewhere warm and dry for a year or so. It will lose about half its weight as it dries. Then soak it in preservative. Don't brush it on, immerse it for a few days so it soaks in where the water used to be.

CHAPTER 10

TOOLS (BASIC)

HAND TOOLS

There's no getting away from the fact that you do need some basic tools, but they needn't cost you too much. Second-hand 'oldies but goodies' are preferable to new 'cheap and nasties'. Some of my present day tools were my dad's and some of those were his dad's. The essentials are:

Claw hammer – to bash in nails obviously and with a claw to pull them out again. Less obviously you can use it on a cold chisel to cut bricks and chip off mortar. Don't hammer a wood chisel with a wooden handle though, or you'll wreck it. Modern chisels with high-impact plastic handles can be hammered. If you do a lot of chiselling you will need a mallet, but a lump of firewood will do for occasional use.

Screwdrivers – a selection of straight and cross-point drivers to suit various sizes of screws. You can use a small, straight blade screwdriver as a bradawl to make pilot holes for screws, or at a pinch use a bradawl as a small screwdriver.

Steel tape – a tape measure is really invaluable for all measuring and not just for woodwork.

Try square – I picked up a roofer's square many years ago. It's marked off in inches, which is probably why it was cheap, but right angles are still 90°. It gets used for all sorts of big projects; building, woodworking and even laying out beds in the garden.

Planes – are useful for smoothing rough wood, reducing thickness or width and skimming a bit off shed doors and gates that have swollen. A Surform tool will do for small jobs but there's no substitute for a sharp plane if you have a lot of wood to smooth. That said, sharpening them takes time and practice. All the jobs in Chapter 8 use either rough timber that stays rough, or ready planed timber.

Chisels – are a bit specialist, but the fence design (pages 93-94) has halving joints and you will need a chisel for that. A 20mm (¾") bevel edged chisel is suitable, and pretty versatile for other things too.

Saws – a general purpose hand saw will do for most jobs and a tenon saw with a rigid back is useful for cutting joints accurately, but not really necessary for any of the projects in this book.

Clamps – (no. not cramps, those are muscle spasms). Old fashioned G clamps are useful for all sorts of things, but expensive to buy new. If you can't find some old ones then the plastic 'quick action' clamps are OK for light work.

G clamps – have a wobbly plate on the screw that allows them to be used on surfaces that are not quite parallel. It is almost always missing from old ones though, so use a piece of scrap wood between the end of the screw and your work. Even with the plate fitted the clamp will mark your work, so if you are doing quality work, always use scrap wood on both sides.

Sash clamps – are the long clamps used to build things like table tops and doors. You don't need them for anything in this book.

Trowel – for building work you'll need a trowel and a big diamond shaped one is fine for macho bricklayers, but be realistic. If you are only an occasional weekend brickie then get a smaller one and give your wrist a break.

For smoothing concrete a plasterer's steel float is the usual choice, but you can make a wooden substitute if you aren't planning to use it a lot. Likewise, a plasterer's hawk is handy for pointing, but a piece of ply about 25-30cm square will do. To make a handle get a bit of wood slightly bigger than is comfortable in your hand and plane the corners off until it feels right. Then nail it on. (See page 20).

Shovel – you can mix mortar and concrete with a spade, and wash it all off afterwards. But leave a bit on once and it seems to grow every time you use it. A cement encrusted spade isn't ideal for gardening, so it's a good idea to get shovel and save it for any building work.

Level – a spirit level is essential, but you don't have to get one of those two metre long jobs that brickies use. For occasional work a 60cm one is fine. Just use it along with a straight piece of wood to check longer surfaces.

Pick – if you are digging in rough stony ground and uprooting trees and shrubs or ancient fence posts you will need a pick. A mattock is a useful alternative which has a pick on one side and a wide, 50mm or so, adze blade on the other which is handy for chopping tree roots.

Power tools – people have been working wood for millennia, but look in any woodworking magazine and you might think it was essential to have at least half a dozen different machines. Well it isn't! The simple truth is that magazines depend on advertising, and most of the companies selling expensive machines that use disposable cutting tools are able to afford many of the more expensive adverts.

You can do all the jobs in this book with no power tools at all. Not only is it cheaper but the exercise will be good for you. Personally I have a power drill, an ancient jigsaw for cutting curves and an electric chainsaw for logging and any coarse woodwork. We did have a battery powered drill/screwdriver once, but a heavy session of IKEA assembly finished it off. Maybe the professional versions with big heavy batteries are better, but the lightweight amateur jobs are pretty feeble. If you are buying a power drill, get one with a hammer action as drilling masonry without it is hard and slow.

Along with the rocks we acquired a lot of sycamore trees and a few ash with this property. I like trees but they do need managing, and an electric chainsaw is the ideal way to convert unwanted saplings to firewood. I leave any serious felling to a neighbour who has a petrol-driven saw, all the safety gear and a certificate to use it.

Work bench – many years ago a friend of mine was teaching woodwork in London. He had a new boy in the class, recently arrived from India. My friend demonstrated the task they had to carry out then sent the kids back to their benches to get on with it. A few minutes later he noticed the Indian boy was missing and went looking for him. He was sitting on the floor with the wood trapped under his feet whilst he cut a perfect mortise joint in it. His dad was a carpenter and had always worked in this way. My friend explained that in the UK we don't do woodwork like that, we use a bench for the purpose. So the lad climbed up, sat on the bench and carried on.

A few years before the above incident, the same friend and I were students at a teacher training college. The college authorities had unthinkingly arranged the workshop opening hours to clash with those of the Union bar, so in order to keep up with our coursework without sacrificing drinking time we all quickly learned how much it was possible to do on the floor of a student bedroom in the early hours of the morning. It was training that has stood me in good stead over the years.

For most jobs you do need a flat surface, and if you are working outdoors a paved yard isn't ideal. The cheapest solution is a large sheet of chipboard, 19mm (¾") in thickness or thereabouts laid on a lawn, yard or any other reasonably flat space you can find. If necessary use offcuts such as slate, bricks or whatever you have to hand to level the board. You can nail or screw blocks to it to act as stops for planing or using a tenon saw, and use it as a jig for glueing complicated structures by fixing blocks and inserting wedges (see the shutter on page 92). To sand any small parts flat, fix a sheet of glass-paper to the board with drawing pins or staples and simply rub the piece on it.

Some jobs are easier done standing up. Sawing is one of them and for that you need something to rest the wood on. An old stool or chair will do for many things and even 8′ x 4′ sheets of board can be sawn on a chair – if you lie the chair on it's side. If you don't have a suitable stool or chair to hand, you could knock up something from pallet wood and nails in just a few minutes.

An old table makes a reasonable enough workbench, and if it's a bit wobbly just brace the legs with some wood (from a pallet, obviously).

One of the most versatile bits of kit ever invented for the DIY market – and popular with most professionals too – is the 'Workmate'. There have been many different designs over the years and several cheaper imitations, but an old steel framed model is hard to beat – though rather heavy to carry around. The split top functions as a vice, and the better models can even be used with the legs folded to hold large items at a suitable height.

Mortar and Concrete Mixes

Cement Mortar Mixes	*Building sand*	*Concreting (sharp) sand*	*Cement*	*Lime*	*Gravel*
Brick or block walls	5	0	1	1(optional)	
Retaining walls	3	0	1	1(optional)	
Pointing	3	0	1	1(optional)	
Rough stone walling	3	3	1	1(optional)	
Rendering, base coat	3.5	3.5	2	1(optional)	
Rendering, finish	4.5	4.5	2	2(optional)	
Concrete Mix General purpose		2	1		4

CONCRETE AND MORTAR

Mixing It

It probably says something profound about our relationship that my wife once bought me a concrete mixer for my birthday. It certainly says something about me that I've had it eight years and still think it's the best present ever. If you are planning to restore walls, lay concrete terraces, build retaining walls, paths and steps then it's certainly worth getting one.

You can mix small quantities by hand, though. First you need a clean place to mix it. A concrete yard is ideal, but it's unlikely you'll ever get it clean again. A 4' square piece of ply is pretty good, but you could even buy a proper mixing tray or mix it in a steel wheelbarrow. You wouldn't have to bend down so far, but it might be a bit awkward mixing it in the corners.

Mix the dry ingredients first as they weigh less and mix more easily than they do once they are wet. To avoid too much lifting, push the shovel under the mix then twist it to turn the mix over. Keep working it until the mix is all one colour.

If you are using a mixer the same principle still applies. It's always much quicker mixing dry aggregates than wet ones. The second mix is usually a problem though. Unless you clean the mixer really well between loads, the second lot of sand sticks to the sides and doesn't mix well with the cement.

When the dry ingredients are mixed, add the water a bit at a time. It's impossible to measure the water unless you know how wet the aggregates were when you started, so add a bit, mix it and add a bit more as required.

How wet you make your mix depends on what you are doing with it. For building, take hold of a handful and squeeze it. It should be wet enough to stick together in a lump, but not ooze between your fingers or drip water.

Concrete for fence posts and the like an be quite dry. Being underground it won't dry out too quickly and it doesn't need to flow into any intricate shapes. If your soil is damp, and it usually is in the UK, you can actually bed your posts in a dry mix and rely on ground water to activate the cement.

Concrete for paths and patios needs to be a bit wetter so that it will level out easily. As I discovered when I concreted the face of some gabions, concrete to pour into deep and narrow shuttering needs to be a lot wetter than the stuff I made. You live and learn, I guess.

Additives

Old-school brickies add a squirt of washing-up liquid to a mortar mix. Prehistoric brickies used to use soap. During the mix the soap/detergent foams, making microscopic bubbles in the mortar that make it 'fatter', ie. it seems almost greasy and spreads more easily. Unfortunately it is also weaker and more porous. It's banned on most serious building sites, though specialist additives might be specified by a structural engineer. For garden walls you don't really need it and a shovel full of lime is better. See below.

Lime Mortar

Lime mortar went out of fashion around the middle of the last century, ousted by the falling price of cement. Lime is more expensive, and you use a higher proportion of it in the mix. Lime mortar takes an age to harden, and when it finally does it's not as hard as cement mortar. So why use it?

Firstly, many people are compelled to by the planning authorities. If you live in a conservation area it may be a rule imposed on any building work. If you have a listed building which was built using lime then any repairs, restorations or additions will require you to use lime, and probably sand from the same quarry that was used when the house was built.
Secondly, you may want to for aesthetic reasons, even if it's not compulsory. In restorations, or building alongside something old, lime mortar looks right.

Thirdly, it's greener. Burning lime takes less energy than making the equivalent amount of cement. It gives off CO_2 during the process, but then re-absorbs the same amount as it hardens in use.

Finally, being softer it is ideal for use with old, soft bricks or soft stone. A hard cement based mortar doesn't 'give' when the temperature changes, so the whole wall is likely to move a little, and that will crack soft bricks.

De-mystifying Lime

Recent TV restoration programmes seemed to put lime on a par with alchemy as something a bit dodgy from medieval history. It's true medieval buildings were built using lime mortar, and frequently lime-washed too, but the chemistry is basic and not at all magical.

Lime goes though a cycle in production and use, starting and finishing as limestone (calcium carbonate - $CaCO_3$). Limestone is actually made up of skeletal fragments of ancient coral and tiny shellfish, and is mined in many places.

The first stage of production involves burning it. In the past this was done by mixing it with coal in a lime kiln, but now efficient gas-fired kilns are used. Burning drives off CO_2 leaving quick-lime (calcium oxide – CaO). Quick-lime has an amazing affinity with water, reacting quite violently and generating a lot of heat. Handling it is not a great idea as even the sweat on your skin will cause burns.

The next stage is called 'slaking', ie. creating a reaction with the quick-lime and water, to produce slaked lime (calcium hydroxide – $Ca(OH)_2$). Traditionally this was done with an excess of water to create lime putty, a suspension of lime particles in water with a putty-like look and feel that settles with a layer of water on top. In modern production the amount of water used can be precisely controlled to slake the lime, but leave it as a dry powder which is sold as hydrated lime.

Hydrated lime is easier to transport than lime putty, but do buy it from a reputable merchant as it needs to kept dry and air-tight. To make lime mortar you will need lime putty which you can make from hydrated lime as follows.

Put a gallon of water in a plastic dustbin or similar container. Stir it with a long stick while your assistant (or whoever) pours in the hydrated lime. By the time you have added about half a bag it will become difficult to mix, so stop. Leave it to stand, making sure there is a layer of water on top. You can leave lime putty under water indefinitely, and it works better if left for a few weeks before use.

To make lime mortar scoop out some putty and combine it with about twice as much coarse sand (by volume). Don't put it in a concrete mixer as the putty will just form a sand-encrusted ball that rolls around the drum and refuses to mix. Unless you have a proper lime mortar mixer you have to do it by hand with a shovel, turning and chopping the putty until it is completely blended. If you make too much you can store the surplus under water. For short periods you can simply put a sack or sheet over it and keep it damp, but for longer periods it is best kept in a bucket or a bin with a layer of water on top.

The way cement and lime harden are very different. Cement needs water to harden and can harden even under water, which is very handy for bridge foundations and sewers, but it won't harden properly if it dries out before the hardening process is complete.

Lime, on the other hand, will stay putty-like for ever if it is wet. The hardening process occurs in two stages; first the water has to dry out, then the lime reacts with CO_2 in the atmosphere to produce calcium carbonate – $CaCO_3$ which is exactly where we started with limestone. In the UK climate drying can take a while, but fortunately the putty becomes stiffer as it starts to dry, making it possible to carry on building even before it has completely dried. The outside layer starts to harden as soon as it is dry irrespective of the amount of water deeper in the wall. This need to dry makes lime mortar an ideal companion for porous common bricks as the bricks suck out the water and the mortar starts to harden.

Pozzolans

You can speed up the hardening process, and even make lime harden while still damp by adding a pozzolanic material. Typically these contain silica which reacts with the calcium hydroxide to produce calcium silicate. In Roman times they added volcanic ash, ground up broken pottery and brick dust to make the world's first concrete. Clay works too, but more common in the UK at least since industrialisation has been to use ash from domestic fires or industrial processes. If you want to experiment try using equal amounts of putty and ash and leaving out some of the sand.

Cement + Lime Mortars

This gets complex. You can add a smallish quantity of hydrated lime as a powder to a cement-based mortar mix to make it smoother and stickier (fatter) and thus easier to spread on your bricks. Check out the chart above.

Some people believe that you can use cement as a pozzolan in a lime mortar, but what seems to happen here is that the cement behaves like cement normally does and hardens, with little effect on the lime which hardens in its own time. So you get a hard but weak mortar quickly, and a stronger one eventually, but it doesn't have any of the advantages of a proper lime mortar.

Conservation and Listing

If you are working on a listed building or in a conservation area, ignore the above and talk to your council's conservation officer. Many years ago the lord of the manor in my home village had the wall round his park re-pointed. It was about 6 to 7' high and something like 5 miles round. It took a while. Then the council objected to the brilliant white lime mortar and made him do it again in grey. You have been warned!

Concrete

For normal common or garden concrete, a ratio of 6:1 for aggregate to cement is right. If you need it really strong, maybe for a cast lintel or similar, then 4 : 1 is better. To make the rough and ready builder's life easier, builders' merchants usually stock 'ballast', though its name and specifications vary around the country. Basically it's ready mixed sand and gravel in a 1:2 ratio, so you take 6:1 of ballast to cement to make your concrete.

In some areas ballast is described by the grading applied at the gravel pit. '20mm all-in' means that everything from sand to pebbles 20mm across is included. That's OK for paths, yards and foundations. If you are doing something thinner then '6mm all-in' is better. If you can't get it, mix 6mm gravel 'pea shingle' with concreting sand.

Some merchants sell recycled crushed concrete. It's cheaper and 'greener' than new aggregate and perfectly suitable for garden projects. It's not that common though. Most recycling is done on larger sites where the old concrete goes into the foundations of the new building and relatively little seems to make it onto the DIY market. I guess this will change as more of the concrete horrors of the '60s and '70s are pulled down.

INDEX